CONVERSATIONS
WITH THE
GODDESSES

CONVERSATIONS WITH THE GODDESSES

Revealing the Divine Power within You

AGAPI STASSINOPOULOS

ILLUSTRATED BY SARAH WILKINS

Stewart, Tabori & Chang

✦

New York

Project editor: Sandra Gilbert
Designers: John Gray and Alexandra Maldonado
Production manager: Kim Tyner

Published by
Stewart, Tabori & Chang
A Company of La Martinière Groupe
115 West 18th Street
New York, NY 10011

LIBRARY OF CONGRESS CATALOGING-IN-PUBLICATION DATA

Stassinopoulos, Agapi.
Conversations with the goddesses : revealing the divine power
within you / Agapi Stassinopoulos ; illustrated by Sarah Wilkins.
p. cm.
Includes index.
ISBN 1-55670-942-0
1. Goddesses, Greek—Psychology. 2. Women—Psychology. I. Title.
BL795.G63 S73 1999
292.2'114—dc21
99-37023
CIP

✦

Printed in Hong Kong

10 9 8 7 6 5 4 3

We never know how high we are
Till we are asked to rise
And then if we are true to plan
Our statures touch the skies—

—Emily Dickinson

For my mother, Elli,
who never put ceilings on my sky,
with my love and gratitude

Acknowledgments

Writing this book has been an incredibly creative and rewarding experience for me. This process could not have taken place without my friend Jane Lahr. Jane collaborated with me on a proposal for a book based on my one-woman show, *Conversations with the Goddesses.* Her aesthetic sense, unerring eye, and expertise gave the book structure and brought it to life. For her passionate commitment to the book and her belief in me, I am forever grateful. This book would not exist without her.

It was Lena Tabori who first supported this book idea and brought me to Jane. Her encouragement, commitment, and valuable insights continued all the way to the end. I deeply value her friendship.

Joan Witkowski, my soul sister, introduced me to Lena, read all the chapters as they were written, and brainstormed with me on every aspect of the book. Our conversations would begin: "How is Demeter?" or "How is Aphrodite?"depending on which chapter I was immersed in. The enthusiasm she shared with me every step of the way was priceless.

Joan introduced me to Stephaney Lloyd. She stepped in with great eagerness, making invaluable recommendations in phrasing and structure. Thanks to her, my office became a safe haven, where, in the constant process of writing and rewriting, I could try anything. My love and gratitude go to her for the devotion she showed in seeing this project to completion.

A big "thank you"goes to Leslie Stoker, the publisher of Stewart, Tabori & Chang, who embraced the project and gave it a home. She brought me to my wonderful editor, Sandy Gilbert, who took great care to keep my voice intact and allowed me to feel completely safe. I greatly appreciate her skillful editorial direction. Sandy found Sarah Wilkins, who drew the symbols so beautifully, and Barbara Clark, the copy editor, who, with all her sensitive and creative suggestions, brought the chapters to a new level of clarity and connection. And thank you also to Helene DeRade Campbell at Stewart, Tabori & Chang, who brought her insightful comments to the project, and to Hilary Ney who generously helped with the book's finishing touches.

I felt surrounded by the love of my friends, who became my cheerleaders: Ron and Mary Hulnick helped me plant the seed for this book by believing in me years ago at the University of Santa Monica; Susan Valaskovic, in Washington, D.C., made very helpful comments; Sandy Forsyth, in London, encouraged me all the way; Margo Marbut contributed her insightful thoughts; Jane Lahr's daughter, Maya, helped with typing in the beginning; my sweet cousin, Mae Georgiadis, was willing to do anything to help me, from picking up a book and making a photocopy to bringing me cappuccino; and Lina and Niko Hiras helped me recharge with coffee breaks and late dinners—a Greek custom. My heartfelt thanks goes to Caryn Kanzer, Leigh Taylor-Young, Ingrid Avallon, Jan Shepherd, Heide Banks, Myra Bairstow, Alexandra McMullen, and Judi Goldfader for all their support. And thank you to my agent, Jan Du Plain, from International Speakers Bureau, for her continuing enthusiasm; to John-Roger, who has graced my life with his friendship; to my father, Costas, who lovingly encouraged me and taught me how to dare; and to my nieces, Christina and Isabella, who keep my heart tender and teach me to ask for what I want. And last—but really first—thank you to my sister, Arianna, who has carved the way for me, protecting me with her canopy of love.

Contents

Greek names are used for chapter titles with Latin names in parentheses.

PREFACE

y love for the goddesses began when I was a child. From the time I was five years old, my mother read the stories of the Greek myths aloud to me and my sister, and my father took us to the ruins of the temples at Olympia, Corinth, and Epidaurus. As I looked at the statues of the goddesses there, I felt their presence larger than life.

Who are the goddesses of the Greek myths, and why should we want to converse with them? In my view, they represent aspects of our own psyche that form part of the collective unconscious. For example, why is it that some women, from an early age, think only of a career—becoming a doctor, teacher, athlete, or businesswoman—while others single-mindedly aim to get married and have a family—or, at the other end of the spectrum, pursue romantic adventures and never settle down? These choices represent qualities associated with the goddesses. Each of us has aspects of all seven goddesses in her personality; some women may have more of Demeter than of Athena, and some women may be more Aphrodite than Hera. But to achieve a healthy balance we all need to integrate characteristics of each of the goddesses into our lives. Understanding these characteristics gives us greater freedom to explore parts of ourselves that may be dormant. The goddesses remind us that we have many possibilities in life, and we don't have to be stuck in one form of self-expression.

Goddesses have inspired women to greater self-awareness for hundreds of years. And great women throughout history—from Cleopatra and Marilyn Monroe to Amelia Earhart and Jane Goodall, from Susan B. Anthony and Eleanor Roosevelt to Florence Nightingale and Mother Teresa—have embodied different aspects of the goddesses. Throughout the ages, women have looked to mythological models for parallels of their own experience. As Joseph Campbell says in *The Power of Myth:* "All the gods, all the heavens, all the worlds, are within us. . . . People say that what we're all seeking is a meaning for life. I don't think that's what we're really seeking. I think that what we're seeking is an experience of being alive . . . "

By identifying the qualities of the goddesses in ourselves, we can recognize needs we have left unfulfilled; by attending to those needs, we can become more self-confident. Through Aphrodite, for example, you can recognize your beauty and claim it as your own. Aphrodite allows our passion to come through and teaches us that we all deserve to love and be loved as women. Following Artemis, we learn to set our boundaries, aim for our goals, and connect with nature. Athena shows us how to develop wisdom and leadership skills, how to excel in a man's world, and how to overcome obstacles. Demeter helps us discover our nurturing qualities. Through Hestia, we learn to live from the center and enhance our spirituality. Hera empowers us to cultivate our partnerships with others. And, finally, Persephone brings us in touch with the deepest parts of ourselves, showing us how to embrace the darkness and transform it into light.

As I move through different stages of my life, different goddesses come to the forefront. I first encountered Aphrodite when I was studying acting at the Royal Academy of Dramatic Arts in London. I was playing the part of Phaedra, a woman in her forties who lusts after her much younger stepson. I was only twenty years old and understood very little about such feelings, but when I cried out to Hippolytus, "Well, then! Know Phaedra and her raging heart. I love you," I was shocked to realize how much passion I had hidden away. All my unexpressed emotions came spilling out, and I was grateful to my art for providing an outlet for my buried emotions.

As I became more immersed in the theater, I realized that other characters from dramatic literature also embodied personality traits of the goddesses. Joan of Arc—a mere girl of sixteen, a virgin, leading a military charge and willing to be burned at the stake for her views—is the perfect example of the Athena archetype. The heroine of Ibsen's *A Doll's House*, Nora, is compelled by Athena to experience an intellectual and social awakening. Antigone, an extremely independent character who defies her uncle's authority, personifies Artemisian qualities. Portia, Brutus's wife in Shakespeare's *Julius Caesar*, urges her husband to confide in her and is, like Hera, a devoted and fiercely loyal spouse. In Tennessee Williams's *The Glass Menagerie*, Laura, an innocent young girl stuck in her own world of darkness, reminds us of Persephone. And Isabella, from Shakespeare's *Measure for Measure*, a pious nun who tries to save the life of her brother, exemplifies Hestia. I was in my twenties when I saw how some part of me could relate to each one of these characters, and to many others.

When I moved from London to Los Angeles, Persephone helped me discover parts of myself that I had hidden under the surface. My need to continue these explorations—to find my own voice—led me to go back to school and obtain my master's degree in psychology. Aphrodite took me completely by surprise again—doesn't she always?—when I fell in love with a man who seemed to fulfill my every need. I felt expanded, joyful, and alive. When the relationship ended, I had trouble letting go and went through a painful healing process. I don't think I could have pulled through without the wise counsel of Athena, who provided me with a new perspective about relationships. Artemis was on hand as well, giving me a new focus on my professional life: it was then that I started work on my one-woman show—*Conversations with the Goddesses*—on which this book is based. Finally, with the help of Hestia and Demeter, the balance of giving and receiving in my relationships was restored.

To fully honor, respect, and value your identity as a woman is to know your own value and command your own power. No one can take that power and knowledge away from you. As Orinthia says to King Magnus in George Bernard Shaw's *The Apple Cart*, "But do not pretend that people become great by doing great things. They do great things because they are great, if the great things come along. But they are great just the same when the great things do not come along . . . It is what I am, not what I do, that you must worship in me." Most of us feel that our accomplishments must be acknowledged by others before they are valid. We don't feel good inside until we get that acknowledgment. And even though we are entitled to be proud, to feel good, when our success is recognized or when we are praised, we must cherish our inner selves *first*, before others do, if we want to manifest our true greatness. The goddesses empower us to find the richness that is hidden inside and create the outer manifestations of success from it. They help us to know ourselves, to value ourselves, and to express ourselves.

As you embrace the seven aspects of the goddesses within you—strength, nurturing, partnership, love, sacredness, transformation, and freedom—you will find the perfect combination to unlock the vault holding the treasure that is you.

APHRODITE

GODDESS OF LOVE, SENSUALITY, AND BEAUTY

THE Myth

S OME SAY THAT APHRODITE IS THE DAUGHTER of Zeus, king of the gods, and Dione, the goddess of the oak tree. But there is a far more romantic story regarding her birth, one that has inspired poets and artists for centuries. Legend has it that Uranus, the sky god, and Gaia, the earth mother, were so tightly bound together that there was no space or light between them. Their closeness became oppressive to Gaia and she appealed to their children, the Titans, for help. Cronus, the youngest of the Titans and the ruler of time, castrated his father with a sharp sickle his mother had given him and threw Uranus's sex organs into the turbulent Aegean Sea. From these fertile waters, roiling with salty semen and white sea foam, emerged the great, glorious, nude Aphrodite, rising from a scallop shell.

Aphrodite was borne by gentle winds to the island of Cythera, which she found too small for her taste, and from there she journeyed to the hills and valleys of the Peloponnesus. Wherever she stepped, dew, flowers, and sweet grass sprang from beneath her shapely feet, and she instilled a joyous desire for coupling in each creature she encountered. Homer, in his second hymn, describes the effect she had, even on animals:

> BEHIND HER MOVED
> GREY WOLVES, FAWNING ON HER,
> AND FIERCE-EYED LIONS AND BEARS
> AND SWIFT-FOOTED LEOPARDS,
> RAVENOUS FOR DEER.
> SHE FELT JOY IN HER HEART TO SEE THEM,
> AND SHE FILLED THEIR HEARTS WITH LONGING,
> SO THAT THEY ALL WENT IN TWOS
> INTO THE SHADE OF THE VALLEY
> AND MADE LOVE WITH EACH OTHER.

Aphrodite wandered far and wide, eventually arriving at Paphos, on the island of Cyprus, where she was greeted, adorned, and generally pampered by the Seasons. The Seasons implored her to cease her wanderings and stay; in response, Aphrodite chose Paphos as her principal seat of worship. Every spring, she returned there to renew her virginity, bathing in the warm, salty tidal waters that rose and fell with the phases of the moon. These ritual baths were attended by the three Charities, or Graces, who helped Aphrodite emerge from her sacred bath even more radiant and joyful than she was before.

Zeus gave Aphrodite's hand in marriage to Hephaestus, the blacksmith of the gods, son of Zeus and his wife, Hera. Born lame, Hephaestus had been cast out of Olympus by Zeus. He fell into the sea and was rescued by the gentle goddesses Eurynome and Thetis, who raised him in an underwater grotto and fostered his great artistic skill. Most considered it odd that the extraordinarily beautiful Aphrodite should marry the homely smithy, no matter how talented he was. Indeed, Aphrodite's deeply voluptuous nature drew her into many important liaisons outside of her marriage, most significantly with Hephaestus's brother Ares, the great god of war.

Brutal, impetuous, strong, and courageous, Ares was nothing if not exciting. His active, fiery nature was irresistibly drawn to its polar opposite in Aphrodite, the golden goddess. Aphrodite bore Ares three children: Harmonia (Harmony), Demos (Terror), and Phobos (Fear). These children were presented to Hephaestus as his own, for he was not aware of the intense love between his wife and his brother. However, their passion was literally brought to light when, one day, Ares and Aphrodite stayed in bed too late, and Helios, the sun, caught them in an amorous embrace. Helios immediately told Hephaestus, who fashioned an amazing invisible bronze net with which he ensnared the lovers at their next rendezvous. Hephaestus summoned all the gods and goddesses to witness the entwined adulterers. The goddesses declined to participate in the humiliation and stayed home; the gods accepted the invitation, but instead of being wrathful, they were overcome with desire. Hermes, the messenger of the gods, and Poseidon, god of the sea, were especially aroused by the sight of the glorious naked Aphrodite. Nobody was interested in helping Hephaestus revenge the infidelity, so Ares and Aphrodite were released.

Hermes and Poseidon, however, soon got their wish: Aphrodite was happy to sleep with both of them. Aphrodite and Hermes had a child, Hermaphroditus, who was half man and half woman. Aphrodite's affair with Poseidon produced two children, Rhodos and Herophilus. The goddess then took up with Dionysus, the god of wine, and bore him a son, the ugly Priapus, who had an excessively large phallus, and a daughter, Hymen, who was exceptionally beautiful.

Zeus soon tired of Aphrodite's romantic adventures and grew weary of her magic girdle, which caused anyone who came in contact with it to fall in love with the wearer. To humble her, he made her fall deeply in love with a mortal—the handsome Anchises, a prince whose beauty rivaled that of the immortals. The goddess came to the hut of his shepherd on the slopes of Mount Ida in Troy. She was beautifully disguised as a princess in radiant red robes, and she seduced Anchises that very night. In the morning, she decided to reveal her identity, but Anchises was terrified. Punishment for any mortal having intimate relations with a god or goddess was certain death. Aphrodite consoled him, telling him they would have a son who would become famous, but warned him that he should tell no one of their night together. Predictably, however, when Anchises was out drinking with his friends, he bragged of his liaison with the goddess. Zeus overheard his boasting and hurled a thunderbolt at him, which crippled Anchises but did not kill him. The son that Aphrodite had spoken about was Aeneas, the hero of the Trojan War.

Aphrodite's other important lover was Adonis, who was born out of an incestuous affair that she inspired. When Adonis's mother, Myrrha (also called Smyrna), boasted that she was more beautiful than Aphrodite, the goddess caused her to fall in love with her own father, whom she deceived and seduced. Myrrha's father discovered the deception and became so enraged that he chased his daughter into the woods and threatened her with a sword. At the crucial moment, Aphrodite changed Myrrha into a myrrh tree, and from that tree Adonis was born. When Adonis was killed by a wild boar, Aphrodite transformed his blood into fields of bright crimson anemones, which flower in the early spring each year.

THE SYMBOLS

SWEET FRUIT
Fruit is the consummation of a natural process in plants; as a symbol, it is the consummation of lovemaking. The sweeter the fruit, the sweeter the lovemaking.

DOLPHIN
This sleek and slippery mammal symbolizes playfulness and the productivity of the sea.

Gold coins

These tokens symbolize richness, fullness, and satiation. Anyone who has true love has riches beyond compare.

Scallop shell

The scallop shell, a symbol of femininity, also symbolizes the intimate parts of a woman's anatomy.

Swan

This graceful bird with the slender, sinuous neck symbolizes elegance and beauty. The soft down of the swan reminds us of all things sensual, like Aphrodite's presence.

Myrrh

Myrrh, a well-known aphrodisiac that is also used in the making of perfume, symbolizes one of Aphrodite's primary pleasures—fragrance.

THE ARCHETYPE
THE POWER OF LOVE

APHRODITE—THE LOVER, THE GOLDEN GODDESS of beauty, femininity, and unrestrained sexuality—blesses us with her gifts of all-consuming passion, charisma, self-assurance, laughter, radiance, grace, and vulnerability. She enhances physical pleasure with incense, oils, and aphrodisiacal food and drink. She enriches beauty with fragrances and cosmetics. Everything that delights the senses is ruled by her.

She also exerts a strong influence over nature: fierce animals become tame for her; small birds circle around her. Flowers and fruits are part of her domain, and she is often described as "garlanded." The ancient Greeks believed that, when Aphrodite was born, a plant that had never been seen before appeared on the earth. The gods dropped nectar on its cuttings and roses were created. Smelling a rose puts us in touch with the simple sweetness inside ourselves, the existence of which we often forget. To invoke Aphrodite is to open ourselves to worlds of exquisite experience.

One of the most famous Aphrodite archetypes is Cleopatra, the powerful queen of ancient Egypt. Legends of her beauty are often disputed. Some claim that her seductiveness lay not in her beauty but in her presence—her beguiling voice, her vivacity, her intelligence. Her irresistible charm was enhanced by beautiful clothes, cosmetics, perfume, and jewels. She was intoxicated by living.

Aphrodite's primal energy fuels the sensual enjoyment of life and the magnetic power of attraction to the beautiful things in it, especially the attraction between two opposite forces: male and female, sky and ocean, sunrise and sunset. Emily Dickinson understood this power and expressed it beautifully:

> OH THE EARTH WAS MADE FOR LOVERS, FOR DAMSEL,
> AND HOPELESS SWAIN,
> FOR SIGHING, AND GENTLE WHISPERING, AND UNITY
> MADE OF TWAIN . . .
> THE BRIDE, AND THEN THE BRIDEGROOM, THE TWO,
> AND THEN THE ONE . . .

Of course, Aphrodite also fuels the libido, and is best known as the goddess of sexual love. She awakens our erotic feelings, which D. H. Lawrence described so powerfully in *Lady Chatterley's Lover:*

> RIPPLING, RIPPLING, RIPPLING, LIKE A FLAPPING
> OVERLAPPING OF SOFT FLAMES, SOFT AS FEATHERS,
> RUNNING TO POINTS OF BRILLIANCE, EXQUISITE,
> EXQUISITE AND MELTING HER ALL MOLTEN INSIDE . . .
> SHE FELT THE SOFT BUD OF HIM WITHIN HER STIRRING,
> AND STRANGE RHYTHMS FLUSHING UP INTO HER WITH
> A STRANGE RHYTHMIC GROWING MOTION, SWELLING
> AND SWELLING TILL IT FILLED HER ALL CLEAVING CON-
> SCIOUSNESS . . . HIS LIFE SPRANG OUT INTO HER.

When we fall in love, our whole identity changes. That is why Aphrodite is called an alchemical goddess: when we love another person, we undergo a metamorphosis. We see the world through different eyes. We feel alive and alert; new sensations and emotions fill our bodies, minds, and souls. We see magic in the world where we saw none before. We vacillate wildly from emotion to emotion, from terror to ecstasy to serenity and back again. Being in love feels like a spiritual awakening: we are drawn out of isolation, humbled, and enveloped by a force greater than ourselves. At the same time, we expand; we feel larger than we were before. Falling in love can be a stepping stone on the way to the awareness of divine love.

The comparison between the physical union of two people and the spiritual union of the human soul with God goes back as far as the Bible. It is uncanny to see how the *Song of Solomon* is filled with aphrodisiacal images.

> THOU HAST RAVISHED MY HEART WITH ONE OF
> THINE EYES . . . HOW FAIR IS THY LOVE . . . HOW
> MUCH BETTER IS THY LOVE THAN WINE! AND THE
> SMELL OF THINE OINTMENTS THAN ALL SPICES!
> THY LIPS, O MY SPOUSE, DROP AS THE HONEYCOMB;
> HONEY AND MILK ARE UNDER THY TONGUE . . .

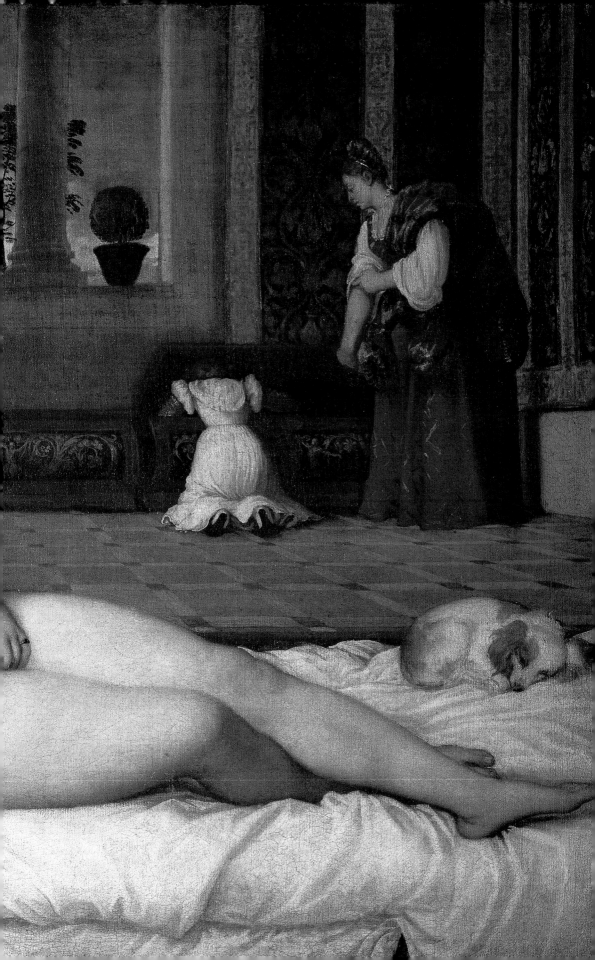

The notion that the body is a temple, the repository of the sacred, is not new. Mystics have told us that the body contains the energy of the soul. Appreciating the capacity for physical love is every person's divine gift. The sixteenth-century Indian poet Mirabai gently encourages us to find that innate divinity:

> O FRIEND, UNDERSTAND: THE BODY
> IS LIKE THE OCEAN,
> RICH WITH HIDDEN TREASURES.
>
> OPEN YOUR INMOST CHAMBER AND LIGHT ITS LAMP.
>
> WITHIN THE BODY ARE GARDENS,
> RARE FLOWERS, PEACOCKS, THE INNER MUSIC;
> WITHIN THE BODY A LAKE OF BLISS,
> ON IT THE WHITE SOUL-SWANS TAKE THEIR JOY.

Feelings for a beloved person can also overflow into other areas of life. We may feel more energized at work or inspired to be more generous toward other people. Love also inspires us to be creative, and creativity is a force as powerful as love. It's no surprise that so many poets, painters, writers, and dancers see Aphrodite as the gateway to an ecstatic union with creativity. She has fired the imaginations of such artists as Walt Whitman, Georgia O'Keeffe, William Shakespeare, and Isadora Duncan. Creating, like love, is directly connected to our souls. The erotic impulse and the creative impulse are inextricably intertwined.

For me, Aphrodite's creative energy is most present when I'm performing. I feel my heart open; I want to give the audience everything. I want them to experience the joy, beauty, and spirit of the goddesses. And at the end of a performance, I feel a deep sense of fulfillment.

The woman who fits the Aphrodite archetype is sensuous and very comfortable in her body, no matter what her shape or size. She is uninhibited in her sexuality, like the speaker in Lucille Clifton's poem "homage to my hips":

> THESE HIPS ARE BIG HIPS
> THEY NEED SPACE TO
> MOVE AROUND IN.

THEY DON'T FIT INTO LITTLE
PETTY PLACES. THESE HIPS
ARE FREE HIPS.
THEY DON'T LIKE TO BE HELD BACK . . .
THEY GO WHERE THEY WANT TO GO . . .
THESE HIPS ARE MIGHTY HIPS.
THESE HIPS ARE MAGIC HIPS.
I HAVE KNOWN THEM
TO PUT A SPELL ON A MAN AND
SPIN HIM LIKE A TOP!

The Aphrodite woman has an innate rapport with the opposite sex. Men are drawn to her like bees to the flowers. Such a woman is completely attentive to the man she is with, and concentrates her feminine energy wholly on pleasing him. Her power lies in her total enjoyment of the process of seduction.

Courtesans throughout history have always enjoyed Aphrodite's special protection. A courtesan, or *hetera* (the Greek word for "other woman"), made the most of her Aphroditean qualities. Courtesans inspired men sexually and creatively and were well paid for it—with jewels, money, and works of art. They were talented lovers, musicians, dancers, and conversationalists. They had more freedom than wives did in the patriarchal society of ancient Greece. Although courtesans were, technically, in bondage to men, they commanded the attention of men of power and frequently used their wages to subsidize the arts. It is said that the great Greek courtesan Rhodopis, with her legendary wealth, was responsible for the construction of an Egyptian pyramid. Aspasia was certainly one of the most influential courtesans of all time, serving as lover, friend, and confidante to Pericles, who is said to have relied on her advice concerning military policy more than on the advice of his lieutenants.

These gifted courtesans turned their ability to attract men into an art form. The power of a courtesan to change the course of history is supported by many examples through the centuries: Mata Hari, who caused countless deaths in World War I by betraying French secrets to the Germans; Christine Keeler, whose affair with cabinet minister John Profumo nearly brought down the British government in the 1960s. The careers of numerous politicians—including Wilbur

Mills, Wayne Hays, and Gary Hart—were almost aborted by their fascination and involvement with Aphroditean women. Literature, as well, is filled with examples of powerful courtesans, such as Anna Karenina, Madame Bovary, and Camille.

But there is a dark side to a man's relationship with a courtesan. Many men feel guilty about the pleasures they enjoy with such women. And sometimes they turn against their mistresses. Often, these men project their own anxieties—psychological, professional, and social—onto the women they are involved with. Veronica Franco, a witty, intellectual writer and a sixteenth-century Venetian courtesan, was brought before the Spanish Inquisition and tried as a witch because of her power to put men "under her spell." In the film *Dangerous Beauty*, based on her life, Veronica eloquently defends herself at her trial:

> I CONFESS I BECAME A COURTESAN, TRADED YEARNING FOR POWER, WELCOMING MANY RATHER THAN BEING OWNED BY ONE. I CONFESS I EMBRACED A WHORE'S FREEDOM OVER A WIFE'S OBEDIENCE. I CONFESS I FIND MORE ECSTASY IN PASSION THAN IN PRAYER. SUCH PASSION IS PRAYER. I PRAY STILL TO FEEL THE TOUCH OF MY LOVER'S LIPS, HIS HANDS UPON ME, HIS ARMS ENFOLDING ME . . . I CONFESS I HUNGER STILL TO BE FILLED AND ENFLAMED, TO MELT INTO THE DREAM OF US BEYOND THIS TROUBLED PLACE, TO WHERE WE ARE NOT EVEN OURSELVES . . . IF I HAD LIVED ANOTHER WAY—A CHILD TO A HUSBAND'S WHIMS, MY SOUL HARDENED FROM LACK OF TOUCH AND LACK OF LOVE—I CONFESS SUCH ENDLESS DAYS AND NIGHTS WOULD BE PUNISHMENT FAR GREATER THAN ANY YOU COULD METE OUT.

Veronica was acquitted because she stated openly the truth of women's lives and because one of her inquisitors was also one of her patrons.

In patriarchal society, where property and the titles of nobility passed from father to son, guaranteed paternity was of primary importance. If a man's wife was sexually attractive—or attracted—to other men, he could not be sure that his children were legitimate. A wife's fidelity was therefore of the utmost importance. Since the children of a courtesan had no status, it was permissible for her to express her sexuality. Even now this reasoning leads many men to have both a wife and a mistress—the former for procreation, the latter for pleasure.

The Aphrodite woman's sex appeal has often been exploited in Hollywood movies. Jean Harlow, Lana Turner, and Marilyn Monroe are just a few examples of the Aphrodite archetypes whose beauty and sensuality were celebrated on film. But, like the life of a courtesan, the life of a sex symbol has a dark side. The beloved Marilyn Monroe battled many demons, including a diminished sense of self-worth. She once said, "A sex symbol is a thing, and I'm not a thing." When the power and beauty of love turn into male fantasies of short-lived sexual pleasure, we enter the world of pornography—an empty shell, where true feeling is suppressed and hollow sensation is glorified.

Aphrodite is called Virga Intacta (an intact virgin, despite her association with sexuality) because every spring she renewed her innocence and virginity in a sacred bath. Thus, every time she couples with a man, she wholeheartedly gives herself anew. Each amorous encounter is fresh, innocent, as though she were falling in love for the first time. She refuses to form a permanent attachment with anyone. Her erotic nature drives her; she applies no boundaries or taboos to her sexual activity. The dark side to this freedom is that a woman who is constantly seeking immediate gratification can end up feeling depleted, hollow, and lonely. Ultimately, she may want a more lasting relationship.

On the other hand, if we banish Aphrodite's influence from our lives we feel bereft and dry—as if all the sweetness of life has gone away. A marriage without sensuality is dull and stagnant. If you judge yourself to be unattractive, if you reject your passionate side, or if you see beauty as only skin deep, life will be colorless. When a woman allows herself to be loved, with all her imperfections—and when she loves a man for who he is, not for who she wants him to be—she awakens the Aphrodite within and opens the door for true fulfillment. Instead of seeking or submitting to power, the true Aphrodite woman recognizes her own, and inhabits her inner paradise.

How to Get in Touch with Aphrodite

 ## Reveal Your Inner and Outer Beauty

◆ Practice the following visualization exercise as often as you can: choose a quiet time when you will be uninterrupted and a place where you can sit comfortably. Inhale deeply and exhale with a big sigh. Do this a few times until you are very relaxed and breathing deeply. Imagine that you are going scuba diving. Expert divers are with you to help you travel into the depths of the ocean. It is a safe trip where you'll be protected and guided along the way. Visualize yourself putting on your oxygen mask and dropping under the water, going deeper and deeper toward the bottom of the ocean. There, you come upon a large, shining chest. With the help of your fellow divers, you bring it to the surface, where it pops open to reveal a most beautiful, radiant, glowing model of you. As you usher your other self out of the waves and onto the shore, the model breathes the fresh air and comes to life. You are faced with a replica of yourself that has your exact shape and looks exquisitely beautiful, radiating love and vulnerability. Your skin is soft and tender; your expression is serene and gracious. There is golden light all around you. Take off your scuba gear and walk hand in hand with yourself up the beach. As you breathe in and out, while walking gently on the beach, this beauty envelops you completely. Allow this experience to help change the way you walk, the way you hold yourself, the way you breathe, and the way you feel about yourself. As you breathe in and out, become comfortable with the knowledge that you are beautiful. See the world with new eyes. Feel the joy of reuniting with a long-lost friend. When you open your eyes, you may think that this new feeling will leave you, but if you often take a moment to revisit that beach and anchor your beauty in your heart, you might experience profound changes in your self-image and in the way others respond to you. What you can behold you can become. (A suggestion: record the steps to this visualization exercise on tape.)

✦ Display a picture of yourself that you love in a prominent place in your home, where you can see it every day; send it loving thoughts.

✦ Treat yourself to a complete makeover. Have a makeup artist do your makeup and photograph the results or take advantage of the free makeovers at your local department store. Experience yourself looking your best.

✦ Go to an elegant shop and try on the most beautiful gowns available. Look at yourself in the mirror and try to form a new image of yourself as beautiful, and worth the expense.

✦ Buy yourself a luxury item you can afford: beautiful lingerie, elegant slippers, an exquisite scarf, or a new perfume.

 PAMPER YOUR BODY

✦ Treat yourself to a day at a spa or beauty salon, where you can indulge yourself with a massage, facial, herbal wrap, or milk bath.

✦ Decide to spend a day in bed without guilt. Have breakfast in bed. Read your favorite books or magazines. Listen to soothing music. Dream.

✦ Take a long, scented bubble bath. Fill the bathroom with candle-light and music you love.

◆ Dance, dance, dance. Belly dancing is a wonderful way to free your hips, but any kind of dancing—from flamenco to tango to salsa to disco—can put you in touch with your body's sensual rhythms.

 ## CHANGE YOUR ROUTINE

◆ Your bedroom is your sacred, aphrodisiacal sanctuary. Introduce more sensual elements into the decor—satiny fabrics, small pillows, scented candles, pictures of romantic places, perhaps even a picture of Botticelli's *The Birth of Venus.*

◆ Design an aphrodisiacal evening with your husband or lover. Share a luscious meal, candlelight, and relaxing music. Wear your softest, most sensual clothes.

◆ Take your time in whatever you do. Rushing cuts off your sensuality.

◆ Ask yourself, "What can I do to incorporate more of Aphrodite in my life?" Write down the answers that surface in your mind. Allow them to be personal and specific.

◆ Write down your feelings about doing things that please you. Do you normally judge yourself as unworthy of experiencing pleasure? If so, you may want to trace these judgments back to your childhood. How did your parents behave with each other? How did they behave with you? If you have negative thoughts and beliefs about pleasure, replace them with positive affirmations—e.g., "I give myself permission to feel beautiful, lovable, and sensual, and to do those things that please and delight me."

A Literary Reflection

Give me a goddess's work to do; and I will do it. I will even stoop to a queen's work if you will share the throne with me. But do not pretend that people become great by doing great things. They do great things because they are great, if the great things come along. But they are great just the same when the great things do not come along. If i never did anything but sit in this room and powder my face and tell you what a clever fool you are, I should still be heavens high above the millions of common women who do their domestic duty, and sacrifice themselves, and run Trade departments and all the rest of the vulgarities.

. . . Thank God my self-consciousness is something nobler than vulgar conceit in having done something. It is what I am, not what I do, that you must worship in me.

. . . Am I not worth it? Look into my eyes and tell the truth. Am I worth it or not?

. . . Everyone knows that I am the real queen. Everyone treats me as the real queen . . . I am one of Nature's queens; and they know it. If you do not, you are not one of Nature's kings.

—Orinthia, the mistress to King Magnus,
in George Bernard Shaw's *The Apple Cart*

ARTEMIS
Goddess of the Hunt,
Wildlife, and independence

THE MYTH

RTEMIS, TWIN SISTER OF APOLLO, GOD OF the sun, is the virgin goddess of the moon and the protectress of childbirth. Along with Hestia and Athena, she is one of the three maiden goddesses of Olympus, and her connection with childbirth is just one of the many contradictions associated with her. She is the most complex of the Olympian deities—at once compassionate and vindictive, nurturing and destructive.

As queen of the wilderness, she represents the force of nature, in which the cycle of birth and death continually repeats itself. And while she encourages us to pay attention to our inner selves, she also recognizes our primal need to connect with nature.

Artemis has her sanctuaries in the most remote and lonely places—the solitude of the forest and mountain, the crystal-clear stream, the flower-covered meadow, and the rough, barren mountaintop. Aeschylus calls her "the lady of the wild mountains." It is her influence that gives warm springs their healing properties. The chorus in Aeschylus's *Agamemnon* praises Artemis for her compassion:

> LOVELY YOU ARE AND KIND
> TO THE TENDER YOUNG OF RAVENING LIONS.
> FOR SUCKLINGS OF ALL THE SAVAGE
> BEASTS THAT LURK IN THE LONELY PLACES
> YOU HAVE SYMPATHY.

Artemis also understands the nature of wild animals and birds—the shy deer, the soaring eagle, the strong bear, the swift stag, the running hare, the stubborn boar, the steadfast goat, and the single-minded bull. You will see her racing across the mountains with her nymphs, playing, dancing, rejoicing in the chase, just like many of the animals she loves. In the *Odyssey*, Homer compares a situation in the narrative to a vision of Artemis:

IT WAS JUST SUCH A SCENE AS GLADDENS LETO'S HEART,
WHEN HER DAUGHTER, ARTEMIS THE ARCHERESS, HAS
COME DOWN FROM THE MOUNTAIN ALONG THE HIGH
RIDGE OF TAYGETUS OR ERYMANTHUS TO CHASE THE
WILD BOAR OR THE NIMBLE DEER, AND THE NYMPHS
OF THE COUNTRYSIDE JOIN WITH HER IN THE SPORT.
THEY TOO ARE HEAVEN-BORN, BUT ARTEMIS OVER-
TOPS THEM ALL, AND WHERE ALL ARE BEAUTIFUL THERE
IS NO QUESTION WHICH IS SHE.

Known as the Bear-Mother, Artemis has a fierce exterior, but, like a mother bear, also displays a softer side of herself. Some young girls in ancient Greece spent years in service to Artemis before going off to marry and have children. They wore bear fur and masks, dancing in wild celebration of their own uninhibited youth, and called themselves *arktoi* (female bears).

Artemis's father was Zeus, king of the gods, whose legendary extramarital dalliances produced many offspring. Zeus had an affair with the nymph Leto, resulting in the birth of Artemis and her twin brother, Apollo. When Zeus's wife, Hera, discovered Leto's pregnancy, she became furious, and sent the serpent Python in pursuit of Leto. Hera decreed that Leto should give birth only in darkness. The south wind befriended Leto and carried her on his wings to the island of Ortygia, near Delos, where she found shelter and gave birth to Artemis. Immediately, the infant ferried her mother across the narrow straits to Delos, where, between an olive tree and a date palm, Leto gave birth to Apollo. Miraculously, Leto did not suffer any pains during her nine days of labor. In recognition of Artemis's miraculous help with this painless delivery, women of ancient Greece paid homage at her temple during pregnancy to ensure a painless labor.

When Artemis was thre ears old, Leto took her to Mount Olympus to meet her father, Zeus, who was totally enchanted with his daughter. Putting her on his lap, he asked her what presents she would like. According to Robert Graves, writing in *The Greek Myths,* she responded:

PRAY GIVE ME ETERNAL VIRGINITY; AS MANY NAMES AS
MY BROTHER APOLLO; A BOW AND ARROWS LIKE HIS;
THE OFFICE OF BRINGING LIGHT; A SAFFRON HUNTING

TUNIC WITH A RED HEM REACHING TO MY KNEES; SIXTY
YOUNG OCEAN NYMPHS, ALL OF THE SAME AGE, AS MY
MAIDS OF HONOUR; TWENTY RIVER NYMPHS FROM
AMNISUS IN CRETE, TO TAKE CARE OF MY BUSKINS AND
FEED MY HOUNDS WHEN I AM NOT OUT SHOOTING;
ALL THE MOUNTAINS IN THE WORLD; AND, LASTLY, ANY
CITY YOU CARE TO CHOOSE FOR ME, BUT ONE WILL BE
ENOUGH, BECAUSE I INTEND TO LIVE ON MOUNTAINS
MOST OF THE TIME.

Zeus, like any proud father, smiled at her and said:

WITH CHILDREN LIKE YOU, I NEED NOT FEAR HERA'S
JEALOUS ANGER! YOU SHALL HAVE ALL THIS, AND
MORE BESIDES: NOT ONE, BUT THIRTY CITIES, AND A
SHARE IN MANY OTHERS, BOTH ON THE MAINLAND AND
IN THE ARCHIPELAGO; AND I APPOINT YOU GUARDIAN
OF THEIR ROADS AND HARBOURS.

Artemis thus proved her intelligence to her father by requesting the gift of
independence and adventure.

After paying this call on her father, the goddess then visited the Cyclopes,
huge, monsterlike creatures who were the children of Mother Earth and Father
Heaven, predecessors of the gods. The Cyclopes each had only one eye and lived
on the island of Lipara. Artemis found them hammering away at a horse trough
for Poseidon, god of the sea. She instructed them to instead make her a silver
bow with a quiver of arrows, in return for which she promised them that they
could eat the first animal she brought down with their handiwork.

Artemis simply did not care for men, with the exception of her twin brother,
Apollo, whom she treated as a subordinate. Once, however, she fell in love with
the hunter Orion. She might have married him had Apollo not given her a chal-
lenge. One day, when Orion was bathing in the sea, he swam so far from shore
that he became nearly invisible. Apollo pointed at the distant object floating on
the surface of the waves and dared Artemis to shoot an arrow at it. Tragically,
she aimed well; the arrow pierced her beloved Orion.

As far as other males were concerned, Artemis had a strong need to protect herself against those who came too close. She eluded Alpheus, the river god, by covering herself and her nymphs with mud so he could not recognize them. And the huntsman Actaeon, while hunting with companions, stopped unknowingly at Artemis's favorite spot to drink from a grotto stream. When he spied Artemis bathing there with her nymphs, the goddess threw water in his face, transforming him into a stag. His faithful hounds, urged on by the other hunters, turned on him and tore his heart out.

The only other exception to Artemis's distaste for men was Prince Hippolytus. He vowed fidelity to Artemis, committing himself to a life of chastity and servitude. However, the goddess of love, Aphrodite, resented his lack of interest in love and his sole dedication to Artemis. In revenge, she caused Hippolytus's stepmother, Phaedra, to fall in love with him. Phaedra lied to her husband, Theseus, and said that his son was in love with her. In response, Theseus exiled Hippolytus, and the anguished prince departed on horseback. Subsequently, he was thrown from his horse and died, but Artemis intervened and resurrected him. Removing him from harm's way, she brought Hippolytus to Aricia, Italy, where she changed his name to Virbius. In gratitude, he established a sanctuary in honor of Diana, Artemis's Roman counterpart.

Although Artemis preferred female companions, she punished them if they did not honor her. Chione, daughter of Daedalion, was destroyed because she found fault with Artemis's beauty; Ethemea, wife of Merops, died for failing to offer sacrifices to her. But for the women who remained devoted to her, Artemis provided vital assistance in times of peril. For example, after asking Agamemnon to sacrifice his beloved daughter Iphigenia to her—promising in return to make the wind blow favorably for his fleet—Artemis saved the girl, replacing her with a stag for the sacrifice, and installing Iphigenia as a priestess in her temple.

THE SYMBOLS

SILVER BOW AND ARROW

The silver bow represents the new moon, a symbol of maidenhood. The arrow symbolizes the swift and direct force that turns ambition into action.

BEAR

The bear is a symbol of brute strength; at the same time, the bear also symbolizes warmth and protection as she mothers her cubs.

Hound

This much-loved symbol of hunting travels in packs, as does Artemis with her nymphs.

Moon

The moon is an ancient symbol of virginity, mystery, and intuition. Venturing forth into the moonlit night, the huntress Artemis is led by intuition rather than logic. To evoke moonlight, her priestesses wore white clay masks during their rituals.

STAG

The stag is a symbol of fertility and renewal. Its antlers graphically suggest the tree of life. The stag was also believed to guide good souls to the Elysian Fields, where they enjoyed eternal happiness after their life on earth.

MOUNTAIN STREAM

The swiftly running water is a symbol of purity. Like Artemis, it travels unhindered through virgin forests.

THE ARCHETYPE
THE POWER OF INDEPENDENCE

LINA SZCZEPANOWSKA, A CHARACTER IN GEORGE Bernard Shaw's play *Misalliance,* is the archetypal Artemisian heroine. A swashbuckling pilot, gymnast, and acrobat, she accidentally crashes her plane into the living room of a stuffy, upper-class English family in pre–World War I England. Her body is vibrant, her attitude robust, and her manner vigorous and alive. Lina is totally unfettered by the constraints of "civilization" and defiantly rejects a traditional feminine role. In her pilot's cap, goggles, pants, and bomber jacket, she is the complete opposite of the placid, compliant Englishwoman of that era. She is a free and uncompromising spirit.

> I AM STRONG: I AM SKILLFUL: I AM BRAVE: I AM INDEPENDENT: I AM UNBOUGHT: I AM ALL THAT A WOMAN OUGHT TO BE . . .

This is unmistakably the voice of Artemis. It is a voice that can be heard everywhere—from the wilderness to the cities. It evokes a free spirit that cannot be tamed. Artemis represents the woman whose independent spirit belongs to no one but herself. She is driven by physical energy rather than the mental energy that drives her sister Athena or the erotic energy that drives Aphrodite. As such, she resembles the clear mountain spring tumbling through uncharted lands.

As goddess of the hunt, Artemis encourages us to keep our energy level high. She dances freely with her maidens, bathes with her nymphs, and rejoices in her lean, lithe, athletic body. By day, she protects animals. At night, by the light of the moon, she and her hounds hunt in the forests. She goes forth with courage, armed with bow and arrows, intent upon capturing her prey and achieving her goals—energetic, direct, motivated, yet free.

Throughout history, many strong women have exemplified the Artemisian spirit. As a 1930s aviatrix, the adventurous Amelia Earhart entered a world inhabited exclusively by men. Her poem "Courage" not only exemplifies her but her Artemisian essence as well:

> COURAGE IS THE PRICE THAT LIFE EXACTS FOR GRANTING PEACE.
> THE SOUL THAT KNOWS IT NOT, KNOWS NO RELEASE
> FROM LITTLE THINGS.
>
> KNOWS NOT THE LIVID LONELINESS OF FEAR
> NOR MOUNTAIN HEIGHTS WHERE BITTER JOY CAN
> HEAR THE SOUND OF WINGS . . .

The anthropologist Jane Goodall embodies the Artemisian love of nature and solitude. Leaving traditional society behind, she spent forty years in Gombe, Tanzania, living with the chimpanzees and documenting their amazing similarity to humans.

Artemis is the prototypical virgin, symbolizing purity of soul. She is a virgin not only physically, but psychologically. She is complete within herself. Her power derives from the boundaries she erects around herself. She exists in complete contrast with her opposite, Aphrodite, who represents abandonment of self through physical union with a man. Who else but three-year-old Artemis would ask her father to give her eternal virginity. Unlike other feminine deities, Artemis is not defined by relationships—as Aphrodite is defined by her relationship to her lovers or as Demeter is defined by her relationship to her daughter, Persephone.

If you are a woman who feels complete without a male partner, the Artemisian spirit is dominant in you. Your true relationship is with yourself. The Artemisian woman does not enter into intimate relationships that require her to compromise her essential nature. She is a guiding force for any person who does not know how to set emotional boundaries.

How often have we become vulnerable to the manipulations and influences of others, focusing on them instead of ourselves. How often have we lost our sense of self or gotten involved in adverse situations. For help with this, we can look to Artemis as our role model for defining personal boundaries. For example, some people who struggle with their weight may create a physical boundary of unwanted poundage between themselves and others. Artemis can help us

45

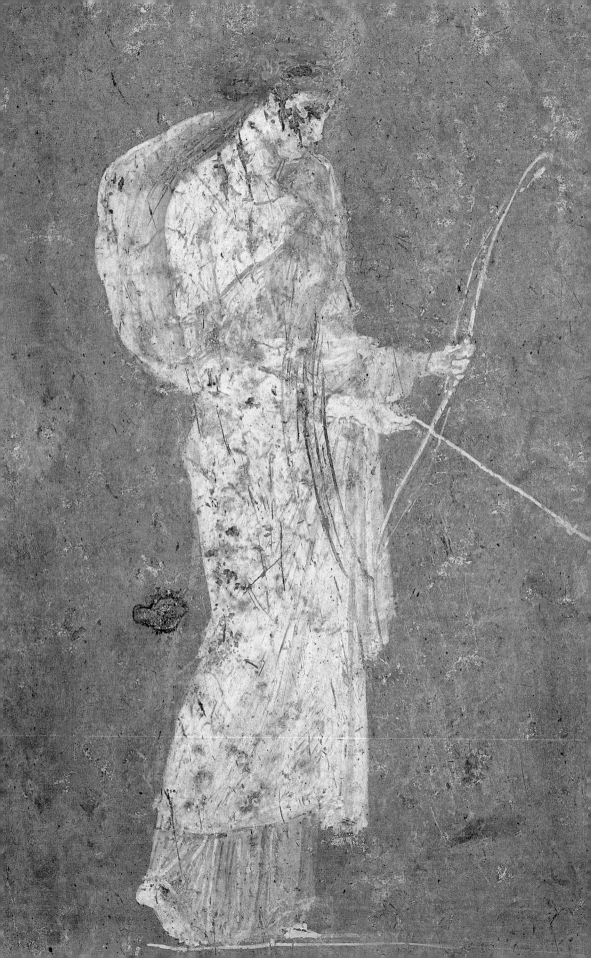

maintain the necessary boundaries without overeating through determination.

I was brought up in a house where boundaries were not clearly defined. I did not know where my sense of self ended and where my perception of others began. I remember visits with relatives and friends during which I was exhausted and depleted quickly because I felt called upon to please everyone. I had not yet learned how to set boundaries to protect myself. It was only later in life that I started to embrace the goddess and say no, establishing my own identity.

Artemis can be a powerful guiding force in our relationships with men. When Artemis interacts with others she does so on her own terms—she remains firm and uncompromised. She never forgets who she is. True Artemisian women have platonic relationships with men. This is not to suggest that you should choose virginity as a way of life, because you must not ignore Aphrodite either. The goal is to integrate your Artemisian spirit with Aphrodite's capacity for love, incorporating the best qualities of both. While Aphrodite is expressing herself, Artemis can maintain your boundaries, resulting in the ability to have balanced relationships with the men in your life—lovers, fathers, brothers, or friends.

Artemis is single-minded—possessing focus, confidence, and independence. Her attitude says, "I can take care of myself." Whenever you find yourself treated with disrespect or condescension, Artemis can help you respond in a forthright manner, assume your strength, and express your honest feelings. If you feel awkward or uncomfortable, she can help you call upon your inner power. You may worry that people will stop liking you or that you might lose your job or that some other calamity will befall you, but why should you accept being mistreated? When you stand up for yourself, especially if you incorporate the diplomacy of Athena, people will respect you for your views. As Eleanor Roosevelt said, "No one can make you feel inferior without your consent."

When you feel the need to be alone, it is Artemis who is speaking to you. Spending time alone enables you to better understand your true nature, and the remoteness often attributed to the goddess is simply part of this personal quest. When you step into Artemis's domain, you commune with your deeper self, the self that is a source of strength and freedom.

The woman who develops the independent spirit and focus of Artemis is a woman who radiates a strong sense of self.

How to Get in Touch with Artemis

Set Your External Boundaries

✦ Learn to establish your physical boundaries. For example, practice the art of graciously saying "no" without feeling guilty.

✦ When the phone is ringing, you don't have to pick it up if you are otherwise engaged.

✦ Choose to spend time with positive people who increase your energy rather than with people who deplete it.

✦ In all your activities, be clear about your purpose and do not be swayed by others' opinions.

Set Your Internal Boundaries

✦ Acknowledge to yourself the things you do well.

✦ Remember that you possess all the inner resources to achieve what you set out to do. Make a list of your short-term and long-term goals and read it out loud. (Hearing your own voice can have a deeper impact than reading in silence.)

✦ Envision your life as you wish it to be. Allow your imagination free rein.

Develop Physical Strength, Vitality, and an Appreciation of Nature

✦ Find a physical activity that you enjoy, such as aerobics, yoga, swimming, tennis, or walking. Experiment to determine which activity suits your lifestyle. Try to engage in some activity on a regular basis, but don't be too hard on yourself.

✦ Make your health a priority. Take direct action to promote your physical well-being. Become aware of what helps you maintain an optimum level of energy.

✦ Leave the city behind, letting nature infuse your spirit. Take walks in the park or hike in the woods.

Develop a Sense of Adventure

✦ Artemis has a deep desire for new experiences, especially those involving the outdoors, friendship with other women, and closeness to animals. List outings you can plan by yourself or with female companions, such as:

    ✦ A "women only" camping trip

    ✦ A trip to a wilderness area

    ✦ Archery lessons

    ✦ Hiking on a nature trail

    ✦ Volunteering at a zoo or an animal shelter

A Literary Reflection

Artemis

I am an honest woman: I earn my living. I am a free woman: I live in my own house. I am a woman of the world: I have thousands of friends: every night crowds of people applaud me, delight in me, buy my picture, pay hard-earned money to see me. I am strong: I am skillful: I am brave: I am independent: I am unbought: I am all that a woman ought to be; . . . And this Englishman! this linendrapper! he dares to ask me to come and live with him in this rrrrrrabbit hutch, and take my bread from his hand, and ask him for pocket money, and wear soft clothes, and be his woman! his wife! Sooner than that, I would stoop to the lowest depths of my profession. I would stuff lions with food and pretend to tame them. I would deceive honest people's eyes with conjuring tricks instead of real feats of strength and skill. . . . I would sink yet lower and be an actress or an opera singer, imperilling my soul by the wicked lie of pretending to be somebody else. All this I would do sooner than take my bread from the hand of a man and make him the master of my body and soul. And so you may tell your Johnny to buy an Englishwoman: he shall not buy Lina Szczepanowska; and I will not stay in the house where such dishonor is offered me. Adieu.

—Lina Szczepanowska in George Bernard Shaw's *Misalliance*

ATHENA
GODDESS OF WISDO
DISCERNMENT, AND LEAD

THE MYTH

THENA, ALONG WITH HESTIA AND ARTEMIS, is one of the three virgin goddesses of Olympus. As one of the most powerful deities, her sphere of influence extends beyond wisdom and leadership to include war and peace, civilization and cities, and arts and literature. Artisans, craftsmen, and tradesmen celebrated her as their teacher and patron, and the women of ancient Greece revered her as the teacher of all women's arts, such as cooking, weaving, and spinning. Athena is said to have invented the plow, the rake, the yoke, the bridle, the chariot, and the ship, as well as the flute and the trumpet. A supreme strategist, Athena is less of a warrior than a protector. Even though she is the goddess of war, she receives no pleasure from battle. Rather, she enjoys her role as a mediator, and prefers to settle disputes by upholding and interpreting the law. Not only do her judgments reveal great wisdom, they show great compassion and mercy as well.

The story of Athena's birth is as dramatic as some of her deeds. Athena's father was Zeus, the mighty king of the gods. One of his first loves was an ocean nymph named Metis. When Metis became pregnant, she told Zeus that the child she was bearing, which she expected to be a boy, would eventually dethrone him. Zeus was not going to take any risks, so he swallowed the pregnant Metis. Soon after, however, he developed such a headache that he asked Prometheus, a Titan, to split open his head to relieve the pressure. From Zeus's split head emerged Athena, fully armed and fully clothed. She instantly became her father's favorite child, the only one who knew where his lightning bolts were hidden and the only one permitted to use his aegis, a magically potent shield. As Homer wrote in his hymn about her:

> PALLAS ATHENA
> I SHALL SING,
> THE GLORIOUS GODDESS

WHOSE EYES GLEAM,
BRILLIANTLY INVENTIVE,
HER HEART RELENTLESS,
FORMIDABLE MAIDEN,
GUARDIAN OF CITIES,
THE COURAGEOUS TRITOGENEIA.

WISE ZEUS GAVE BIRTH TO HER HIMSELF
OUT OF HIS MAJESTIC HEAD.
GOLDEN ARMOUR CLOTHED HER,
WARLIKE, GLISTENING.
ALL THE GODS WHO SAW HER
WERE OVERCOME WITH AWE.

Athena's association with cities in general and Athens in particular began during a dispute on Olympus about who should be the patron god of Athens. In an effort to determine who could provide more benefits to the city, her competitor, Poseidon, god of the sea, opened a well on the Acropolis. In response, Athena planted an olive tree there. Cecrops, the half-human king of Attica, judged Athena's gift to be more valuable, so she became the city's protector.

Athena is perhaps the most benevolent of goddesses. She has very few selfish, ulterior motives, and is almost always totally ethical. Like most of her fellow deities, however, Athena was known to punish those who did not honor her. Arachne, an unfortunate mortal whom some say was a princess and others claim was a simple peasant girl, was extremely skilled in weaving. One day, Arachne wove a cloth of such surpassing beauty that Athena simply could not find fault with it. In a rage, Athena tore the cloth in two. Arachne was so ashamed that she hanged herself, but Athena, perhaps feeling a little remorseful, changed Arachne into a spider, who at least could retain her skill at weaving. Another unfortunate mortal was Myrmex, a former companion of Athena who boasted that it was she, not Athena, who invented the plow. For this indiscretion, Athena changed Myrmex into an ant.

The most famous example of Athena's role as protector is her championship of the Greeks in the Trojan War. She was understandably displeased when Paris, son of the king of Troy, judged Aphrodite to be more beautiful than either Hera or herself. In return, Aphrodite promised him the most beautiful woman in the world, Helen of Troy. Paris's abduction of Helen caused her husband, Menelaus, to call upon all of Greece to rescue her, and thus began the Trojan War, which, with Athena's help, the Greeks eventually won.

Athena became a kind of "cheerleader" for various heroes: she helped Bellerophon capture Pegasus, the winged horse, and put a bridle on him; she helped Perseus slay Medusa, the Gorgon whose head was covered with snakes; she assisted the Argonauts in their quest for the golden fleece. She appeared at the side of Achilles to help him control his passion when he was ready to reach for his sword and slay Agamemnon. She also protected Hercules as he completed his twelve labors, and defended Orestes when he came before the court for his crime of murdering his mother, Clytemnestra. And it was Athena who guided Odysseus in his journey home to Ithaca. As Odysseus remarked in the *Odyssey*: "She always stands beside me in all my tasks and always remembers me wherever I go."

THE SYMBOLS

Olive tree

An olive branch can signify both victory—olive wreaths as well as laurel wreaths adorned the brows of conquering heroes—and peace. Since the Greeks depended on olive trees for food and fuel, the olive tree also symbolizes well-being.

Owl

This nocturnal bird symbolizes wisdom, erudition, and patience. Because of its excellent night vision, the owl sees things in the dark that others can't. The owl also symbolizes discernment.

SHIELD

Athena is rarely depicted
without a shield, the symbol
of protection. The figure on
the shield is the head of
the terrifying Medusa,
which Perseus vanquished
with Athena's aid. It
represents conquering
our deepest fears.

LIGHTNING BOLT

This ancient symbol of
masculine vitality can
also symbolize a sudden
realization or idea. Its
association with Zeus gives
it connotations of power
and government as well.

Loom

The loom represents productivity, strategy, craftsmanship, and the intricacy of thought.

Parthenon

This temple honors Athena and is symbolic of her strength as protector of the city.

THE ARCHETYPE
THE POWER OF THE MIND

ATHENA, BORN OUT OF THE HEAD OF HER FATHER, represents the positive male aspect of ourselves. She is bright-eyed, shrewd, and brilliant; she is resourceful and inventive; she acts as wise counselor and companion to her heroes. As she says in Aeschylus's *Eumenides*, "I love them as a gardener loves his plants, these upright men, this breed fought free of grief." However, her involvement with men is platonic, and Athena remains a virgin, which is precisely the source of her strength.

Athena never worries about stealing a man's thunder; after all, she knows where lightning comes from. She gives women permission to travel in male territory without guilt, fear, or anxiety. She brings mercy, wisdom, and soulfulness into the masculine world, and with it the confidence that a woman is as capable as any man.

The praises of wisdom personified are sung in the Apocrypha:

> FOR IN HER THERE IS A SPIRIT THAT IS
> INTELLIGENT, HOLY,
> UNIQUE, MANIFOLD, SUBTLE,
> MOBILE, CLEAR, UNSPOILED,
> DISTINCT, INVULNERABLE, LOVING THE GOOD, KEEN,
> IRRESISTIBLE, BENEFICENT, HUMANE,
> STEADFAST, SURE, FREE FROM ANXIETY,
> ALL-POWERFUL, OVERSEEING ALL,
> AND PENETRATING THROUGH ALL SPIRITS
> THAT ARE INTELLIGENT, PURE, AND MOST SUBTLE . . .
> SHE REACHES MIGHTILY FROM ONE END OF THE EARTH
> TO THE OTHER,
> AND SHE ORDERS ALL THINGS WELL.

> —*The Wisdom of Solomon* 7:22–23; 8:1

Athena always meets us at our point of greatest need. She instills us with courage, and reminds us that we must be brave. As we undertake a difficult assignment, encounter stumbling blocks along the way, or come up against a wall of doubt, Athena whispers in our ear: "Be strong, and mighty forces will come to your aid."

The Athena archetype, ultimately, demonstrates the virtue of self-government—a higher form of government than that of the state. Athena reasons that if humanity would learn how to govern itself, the world would be a better, more peaceful, and more balanced place. How wonderful it would be if, at the moment we feel ourselves losing control, we could remind ourselves of the wise voice of Athena, urging us to stop and think before we act—just as Athena stayed Achilles's hand when he drew his sword to kill Agamemnon, helping him follow his higher self rather than his wildest passions.

Athena uses her powers of persuasion and her verbal facility to effect justice and mercy for those who have been mistreated, just as Portia, a character in Shakespeare's *The Merchant of Venice*, speaks out on behalf of her beloved Bassanio in court.

Both fictional and historical women throughout the centuries who exemplified the Athena archetype have passionately advocated the idea that women should reach their full potential. They believed that women must not be allowed to stagnate in the limiting roles society has imposed on them. The character of Nora in Ibsen's *A Doll's House*, published in 1879, was the ultimate anti-Athena heroine. However, when her husband told her that "You are a wife, and a mother before everything else," she was propelled by her Athenian courage to reply, "I don't believe that any more. I believe that I am a human being, just as much as you are." As threatening as it may seem, we might have to walk away from our sheltered environment to discover the possibilities life holds for us. Sojourner Truth is another powerful example of the Athena archetype. She transcended sex, color, and slavery to become a fearless advocate of human rights. In 1826, a year before she was freed, according to the provisions of New York law, she escaped from her master and became a traveling evangelist.

My sister, Arianna, has always represented the Athena archetype to me. Ever since she was a little girl, she has demonstrated a tremendous passion for knowledge, always excelling in school and showing maturity, focus, and self-discipline.

She never let major or minor obstacles stand in her way. One morning in 1967, after the military had seized power in Greece, we woke up to find armed soldiers outside our house. Arianna had an afternoon lesson with her economics tutor. Although phone service was cut off and radios were constantly broadcasting warnings that everyone should stay home or risk being being arrested, Arianna refused to be intimidated. She left for her appointment as scheduled. I watched from the window, anxious about what could happen to her. At the corner, soldiers told her she had to return home immediately—and, wisely, she did. However, I never forgot her incredible strength and sense of purpose. Now, as an accomplished writer and columnist, she never hesitates to express her views. Her influence has inspired me to develop my own Athena qualities of self-sufficiency and self-determination.

Often, women who follow the example of Athena demonstrate the goddess's qualities at a young age. When the Russian writer Nina Berberova was asked to pinpoint when she became a liberated woman, she answered: "At eight, it started. At nine. At seven, maybe. I looked around and saw that women with children were silly and boring. That women with a profession were not boring. I decided to have a profession . . . At seven, at eight, I thought, I will grow up and meet interesting people. I will read interesting books. I will write . . . I thought, How wonderful my life will be! . . . I thought that would give me the greatest pleasure in life. And it did!"

The Athena woman comes into her own in the workplace, putting in long hours in the fields of law, science, education, business, or as an agent for political or social change. Highly competent, hardworking, productive, self-assured, logical, interested in the common good, her intellectual strength guides her to powerful positions in which her skills can be utilized and in which she can empower herself to excel. The men around her, who are usually equally powerful, are colleagues and companions, not lovers.

Ruled by her head, not by her heart, the Athena woman may appear unaffectionate, cold, or self-righteous. Athena had no relationship with her mother, and instead embraced her primary connection to her father and the masculine qualities he represents, rejecting the notions of sexuality and marriage. Similarly, the Athena woman carefully guards her intimate side under her shield, protecting her emotions and disguising her vulnerability. If she wants to awaken her unexpressed womanliness, she will have to use the same passion she applies to her intellectual achievements. Just as Athena, the goddess of weaving, combines diverse elements to produce a whole, the Athena woman must integrate her masculine side with her feminine side, her strength with her vulnerability; her creativity with her caring; her self-discipline with her passion; and her intelligence with her imagination. That way, she can enrich the tapestry of her life and work in greater harmony with herself.

The Athena woman's capacity for caring manifests itself as action rather than emotional nurturing. Florence Nightingale struggled with her family for years because, from an early age, she wanted to help those in need and felt that her life had a purpose higher than marriage. In her book *Cassandra*, published in 1852, she speaks about the spiritual and intellectual costs of a woman's domestic confinement: "The family uses people, *not* for what they are, not for what they are intended to be, but for what it wants them for—its own uses. It thinks of them not as what God has made them, but as the something which it has arranged that they shall be." At the age of thirty, Florence Nightingale began making the nursing profession respectable for women. Her standard of nursing care was eventually adopted worldwide.

Women who fit the Athena archetype can also be found in the arts, where they combine their business acumen with creative power. The sculptor Louise Nevelson sacrificed the personal comforts of marriage, family, and financial security for more than thirty years to follow her own artistic vision. Fashion designers like Vera Wang, Donna Karan, and Nicole Miller, among others, use Athena's gifts of inventiveness and self-reliance to build international recognition for their work. The director and designer Julie Taymor brought the musical *The Lion King* to life on stage with her innovative use of puppets and masks. Joan of Arc, as depicted by George Bernard Shaw in his play *Saint Joan,* embodies the characteristics of Athena in her capacity as goddess of war:

> I WILL NEVER TAKE A HUSBAND . . . I AM A SOLDIER: I
> DO NOT WANT TO BE THOUGHT OF AS A WOMAN. I
> WILL NOT DRESS AS A WOMAN. I DO NOT CARE FOR THE

THINGS WOMEN CARE FOR. THEY DREAM OF LOVERS, AND OF MONEY. I DREAM OF LEADING A CHARGE, AND OF PLACING THE BIG GUNS. YOU SOLDIERS DO NOT KNOW HOW TO USE THE BIG GUNS: YOU THINK YOU CAN WIN BATTLES WITH A GREAT NOISE AND SMOKE . . . MY HEART IS FULL OF COURAGE, NOT OF ANGER. I WILL LEAD; AND YOUR MEN WILL FOLLOW: THAT IS ALL I CAN DO. BUT I MUST DO IT: YOU SHALL NOT STOP ME.

Like Athena, Queen Elizabeth I—also known as the virgin queen—surrounded herself with men of great intelligence and talent, and a new literary world blossomed around her. Eleanor of Aquitaine, even though she was imprisoned by her husband, Henry II, refused to submit to him, and inspired other women to strive for political equality with men. Eleanor Roosevelt turned the disappointments in her life into activism, which she pursued to improve the lives of others. Susan B. Anthony, an early suffragette, voted in the 1872 election and spoke in her own defense using rhetorical skills worthy of Athena herself: "It was we, the people, not we, the white male citizens, nor we, the male citizens; but we, the whole people, who formed this Union. . . . It is downright mockery to talk to women of their enjoyment of the blessings of liberty while they are denied the only means of securing them provided by this democratic-republican government—the ballot."

By choosing to act upon the truth, regardless of the circumstances, these historical Athena archetypes have given us true liberation. They inspire us to be who we are without compromise or apology. Athena leads us to a greater sense of inner balance by giving the mind authority over our baser human instincts, leading to a victory for the higher self.

How to Get in Touch with Athena

Identify Your Goals

◆ List goals or experiences that are important to you, which you have contemplated doing but have not accomplished because of fear or doubt. Consider each item on the list and write down the specific reason you have not attempted or finished it. Choose the easiest item on the list and consider doing that one first.

◆ Choose a woman you admire as your role model. Write down in detail all the things you admire about her. Identify the qualities in her that have enabled her to accomplish her goals, and realize that you wouldn't be able to identify them if they weren't also in you!

Define Your Relationship with Your Father

◆ Write a short biography of your father. Describe your relationship to him. Include as much detail as possible. How does he behave with your mother and your siblings? What is he like at work? What is his relationship with money? Does he give you his attention? Admire you? Encourage you? Praise you? Is he generous or guarded with his affection? What about you does he approve of and what does he disapprove of? Is he communicative? Be sure to list both positive and negative traits.

◆ Write a list of all the reasons why you are grateful to your father, and another list of all the things you wish he had done differently. For each item on the latter list, say "I forgive myself for judging my father for . . ." or "I forgive myself for not feeling worthy of my father's love." By beginning each sentence with "I forgive myself," you can take responsibility for the judgments you have made, which you may have held on to for a very long time, and which might still be holding you back from owning your masculine attributes.

Expand Your Mind

✦ Join a book group or start your own.

✦ Learn a new language.

✦ Choose a social issue about which you feel passionate and get involved with organizations devoted to that issue. Go to meetings, read their literature, participate in discussions.

✦ Vote. Your voice counts as much as anyone else's.

A Literary Reflection

The quality of mercy is not strain'd;
It droppeth as the gentle rain from heaven
Upon the place beneath: It is twice bless'd;
It blesseth him that gives and him that takes:
'Tis mightiest in the mightiest; it becomes
The throned monarch better than his crown;
His sceptre shows the force of temporal power,
The attribute to awe and majesty,
Wherein doth sit the dread and fear of kings;
But mercy is above this scepter'd sway,
It is enthroned in the heart of kings,
It is an attribute to God himself;
And earthly power doth then show likest God's
When mercy seasons justice. Therefore, Jew,
Though justice be thy plea, consider this
That in the course of justice none of us
Should see salvation: we do pray for mercy;
And that same prayer doth teach us all to render
The deeds of mercy.

— Portia in Shakespeare's *The Merchant of Venice*

DEMETER

GODDESS OF THE HARVEST

AND FERTILITY

THE MYTH

HE POIGNANT STORY OF DEMETER AND HER daughter Persephone—who is sometimes called Kore, which can mean "maiden," "sprout," and, in modern Greek, "daughter"—is one of the richest, most profound, and moving in all Greek mythology. Mother and daughter are inseparable. They are referred to as "the two goddesses," or "the Demeters," as though the shoot were simply a young form of the mother plant and not separate from it.

Demeter is the daughter of the Titans Rhea and Cronus and sister to Zeus, Poseidon, and Hades—the three brothers who ruled heaven, the sea, and the underworld respectively. She is sometimes associated with Gaia, the earth, who is her grandmother. Demeter represents the earth's fertility and abundance, as well as the many nurturing foods that humans cultivate with her help.

Demeter is also the goddess of plenty. Her presence presides over everything that grows. She gives man the sickle and the plow so that he can live off the earth, which she makes fertile with fruit and grain. The earth is, in a way, her other daughter, and the sheaves of wheat are her sons and mates.

Stories about Demeter apart from her relationship to Persephone are few. However, when she was young, she fell in love with a mortal, Mecon, whom she changed into a poppy, a flower that remained sacred to her from then on. She also fell deeply in love with Iasion, the son of Zeus and Electra, whom she met at the wedding of Cadmus and Harmonia. (The name of their son, Ploutus, means "wealth" in Greek.) Hesiod, in his *Theogony*, written about 800 B.C., describes their courtship:

> DEMETER, SHINING GODDESS, JOINED IN LOVE
> WITH IASION THE HERO, ON THE RICH
> ISLAND OF CRETE. THEY LAY ON FALLOW LAND
> WHICH HAD BEEN PLOUGHED THREE TIMES,
>   AND SHE GAVE BIRTH
> TO PLOUTUS, SPLENDID GOD WHO TRAVELS FAR

OVER THE LAND, AND ON THE SEA'S BROAD BACK;
AND EVERYONE WHO MEETS OR TOUCHES HIM
GROWS WEALTHY, FOR GREAT RICHES COME
FROM HIM.

Soon after Demeter had coupled with Iasion, Zeus—hewing to the tradition that mortal lovers have to die after they mate with one of the gods—struck him dead with a thunderbolt.

Persephone—the greatest love of Demeter's life—was Demeter's daughter by her brother Zeus, who was thus both Persephone's father and her uncle. One of Persephone's other uncles, Demeter's gloomy brother Hades, was very lonely, having inherited the dominion of a sunless underworld. Hades fell in love with his niece Persephone and went to his brother Zeus for permission to marry her. Zeus, afraid of offending his older brother and knowing Demeter would not forgive him if he acceded, agreed to help Hades abduct the girl. While she was picking blossoms in a lush meadow, Persephone saw the narcissus, a radiant flower with an intoxicating fragrance. (Gaia, the earth mother, had created this wonder to please Hades and attract Persephone.) As Persephone reached for the flower, the earth opened beneath her feet and Hades grabbed her. Screaming and weeping, she was carried off to the underworld in Hades's golden chariot, pulled by his immortal horses. One of the earliest Homeric hymns tells us:

AND THE PEAKS OF THE MOUNTAINS AND THE DEPTHS
OF THE SEA ECHOED
WITH HER IMMORTAL VOICE, AND HER QUEENLY
MOTHER HEARD HER.
A SHARP PAIN SEIZED HER HEART.

Demeter tore the diadem from her head, covered herself in dark sheets of mourning, and for nine days and nine nights wandered the earth without eating, drinking, or bathing, searching for her daughter, crying, "Where is my loved one? Wherefore do ye wail?"

On the tenth day, Hecate, goddess of the night, who had also heard Persephone's cries, came to Demeter. Together they went to the god Helios, the

sun, who told them that Zeus helped with the abduction. This plunged Demeter deeper into her grief, and she wandered the earth, searching for solace, hospitality, and a way to get her daughter back from the clutches of Hades. Disguised as an old woman, Demeter eventually arrived at Eleusis, in Mycenae. She came upon King Celeus and his wife, Metaneira, who opened their palace to her and invited her to remain as nurse to their newly born prince, Demophoön. She fed him ambrosia, and breathed on him sweetly as she held him in her lap. At night she held him in the center of a powerful fire, intending to burn his mortality and gradually transform him into a god. His parents were astonished at how quickly he was growing. Demophoön's transformation into one of the immortals would have been complete were it not for Metaneira's worry and curiosity. One night, she spied on Demeter and saw her holding Demophoön over the fire. She screamed, causing Demeter to drop the child in the fire, where he died.

Demeter was furious with Metaneira, blaming her for her child's death. King Celeus, too, was distraught; at this point, seeing his grief, Demeter revealed herself to the couple, throwing away her old woman's disguise and changing her mortal size and shape into an awesome, magnificent presence. Beauty drifted all around her; her blond hair fell around her shoulders, and her brightness shone far and wide. She promised to bring great gifts to the king and queen, including the birth of another son, Triptolemus, whom Demeter would appoint as her special messenger to teach mankind the art of agriculture. She asked the people of Eleusis to build her a huge temple with an altar beneath it. When it was finished, she retreated there alone, mourning the loss of her daughter.

An entire year passed, during which, because of her grief, Demeter let everything on the earth wither and die. Nothing grew; there was no food and nothing to harvest. She was determined to wipe out the whole human race with a painful famine and thereby deprive those who lived on Olympus of all their offerings and sacrifices. Zeus sent every one of the gods to implore her to restore fertility on the earth. When all had failed to move her, he finally relented and sent Hermes, the messenger of the gods, to tell Hades that he must let Persephone return to the daylight world.

Hades could not disobey the command of King Zeus. However, it was well known that anyone who tasted the food of the dead would be bound to return to the underworld. As they were parting, Hades offered Persephone (who had not eaten a morsel during her confinement) some pomegranate seeds. Relieved and joyful that she was going to be reunited with her mother, Persephone swallowed one. Alas, from that point on, she was doomed to spend one-third of the year in misted darkness with Hades, during which time the earth would lie bare and fallow and bleak; the rest of the year, she was free to be with her mother and the other gods, during which time the earth would bloom with fragrant flowers, fruits, grains, and other crops. For at least part of the year, Demeter brought abundance back to the earth.

The worship of Demeter continued at her temple at Eleusis. Because those who performed her rites were commanded to keep them a secret, these rituals became known as the Eleusinian Mysteries, enacted and handed down only by those whom Demeter had chosen. It is probable that these men and women also served as agricultural advisors, showing people how to plant, cultivate, and harvest the precious gifts of the earth.

THE SYMBOLS

The cornucopia is a symbol of abundance, profusion, and the bounty of the fruits of the earth, which Demeter so generously provides for all humans.

POPPY

Symbol of eternal love and transformation, this flower grows freely in fields of wheat.

SICKLE

This agricultural instrument represents productivity and cultivation. It also symbolizes the opposite—the cutting down of new growth—in recognition of Demeter's refusal to make the earth fertile after Persephone's abduction.

SHEAVES OF WHEAT

Wheat, symbolizing the bread of life, nurtures and sustains the body.

GOLDEN CROWN

The golden color of the crown symbolizes Demeter's divine radiance. The crown itself is symbolic of the goddess's reign over the earth's fertility.

TORCH

The constant light of the torch symbolizes hope and faith. Demeter used the torch in her attempt to retrieve Persephone from the underworld.

THE ARCHETYPE
THE POWER TO NURTURE

EMETER IS MOTHER: SHE REPRESENTS THE mothering aspect of ourselves. Whether she literally becomes a mother or not, a woman who fits the Demeter archetype is a nurturer, caretaker, and often a great healer. At the core of Demeter's being is her abundant love and generous heart, which extends to the whole earth—to everything that grows and gives nourishment. She's motivated by the most powerful of instincts—to give life—and is selflessly devoted to the life she creates.

We can only think of Demeter in relationship to her daughter—so strong are their ties. Ancient sculptures of Demeter and Persephone show them looking deeply into each other's eyes—the secret they share through their penetrating gaze is at the heart of Demeter's myth. In the words of Carl Jung: "Every mother contains her daughter in herself, and every daughter her mother, and every woman extends backwards into her mother and forwards into her daughter."

I have been blessed with a mother who embodies the archetype of Demeter. For as long as I can remember, my mother was completely devoted to the wellbeing of her two daughters. In women who fit the Demeter archetype, the instinct to nurture is so deeply ingrained that it overshadows the qualities of the other goddesses. Often, a Demeter woman lacks Aphrodite's passion or Artemis's independence, and neglects Hera's principle of partnership with her husband. It is possible for her to feel contained and fulfilled solely by virtue of her relationship with her children.

Demeter hears the demands of all those around her, even if they are not her children, and feels a compelling need to respond. That is when the Demeter woman is entrapped by her "mother nature." She feels she has to be all things to all people, and her own needs sometimes go unmet. She must learn to say no, and apply Artemis's sense of boundaries and Aphrodite's ability to put herself first, so she can give to others from an overflowing rather than a half-full cup.

Women who personify the Demeter archetype are usually great spiritual leaders who offer strong emotional support. They may choose to become psychotherapists, or to be involved in organizations that strive for the betterment of the human condition. Golda Meir "mothered" the state of Israel and grieved for all its lost children. Maya Angelou, who raised her son by herself, nurtures people through her poetry. Oprah Winfrey brings the spirit of Demeter to life through her television show, giving birth to programming that feeds the minds and souls of her viewers. Anne Sullivan, teacher of the blind, deaf, and mute Helen Keller, who encouraged little Helen to reject the role of outcast and become a prominent citizen and an inspiration to millions, definitely followed the example of this goddess for her outstanding contributions to humanity.

Food is an essential way for the Demeter woman to express her generosity. My mother always offered food to every person who walked into our house. She became very well known among the postmen and the newspaper delivery boys, and enjoyed her reputation as an earth mother. She wouldn't allow any of them to leave without a piece of fruit, a cookie, or a handful of nuts to sustain them on their journey. She always kept a big basket filled with treats on a table in the entrance hall, so that everyone who entered could partake of the bounty. Next to the basket was a large terra-cotta pot containing a sheaf of dried wheat—a symbol of abundance. One of my great joys when I go back to Greece is to be in the company of other women in the kitchen, preparing wonderful meals, baking bread and cookies, feasting with family and friends.

At an early age, I began to exhibit my mother's characteristics, becoming extremely giving and supportive to all those around me. Often, I overextended myself to the point of exhaustion. Even in my relationships with men, I had the tendency to mother them, which of course very quickly killed any romance in the relationship.

One day, I saw a wonderful green T-shirt with the words, "I worship the ground I walk on." That could very well be a quotation from Demeter. I hear her asking us all to honor her earth and to stop depleting its resources. If we could only look at the earth and its wonders through reverent eyes, perhaps we would not be so quick to take it for granted or to waste its gifts. In the words of Kahlil Gibran:

> In a field I have watched an acorn, a thing so still and seemingly useless. And in the spring I

HAVE SEEN THAT ACORN TAKE ROOTS AND RISE, THE
BEGINNING OF AN OAK TREE, TOWARDS THE SUN.

SURELY YOU WOULD DEEM THIS A MIRACLE, YET
THAT MIRACLE IS WROUGHT A THOUSAND THOUSAND
TIMES IN THE DROWSINESS OF EVERY AUTUMN AND THE
PASSION OF EVERY SPRING.

Mankind has deeply dishonored Mother Earth in our efforts to make her
serve us. We have not thought about what she needs in return. We have fallen
out of touch with the sacred (natural) process of nourishment and regeneration,
and we don't recognize the sacred (natural) part of ourselves that is connected
to Mother Earth. I can hear Demeter demanding that Zeus restore her daughter,
the earth, to wholeness. I can hear her summoning us women to help feed her
children. There are 24,000 people on the earth who die of starvation every day,
most of them women and children. If we don't take action to heal ourselves and
the earth, who will?

Demeter undergoes a powerful transformation when Persephone is suddenly
abducted by Hades. She's grief-stricken and devastated by her loss but, unlike
Persephone, she does not remain passive. Instead, she uses her power to take
action. In search of a solution, in search of some comfort, the great goddess
disguises herself as a nursemaid and looks after the son of King Celeus. By
humanizing herself, Demeter starts to undergo the process of transformation.
Later, as an expression of her grief, she causes everything on earth to wither and
die. In a rage, she is prepared to wipe out the human race unless Zeus intervenes.
Ultimately, her experience yields a great benefit to humanity in the form of the
Eleusinian Mysteries and the agricultural instruction offered by her priests and
priestesses.

The loss or death of a child, one of the most devastating things a human
being can experience, can eventually lead to spiritual growth. In fact, any loss
of something that gives emotional value to a woman's life can have the same
effect—children leaving home, the end of a relationship, the loss of a job, a
failed business plan.

The well-known writer Isabel Allende lost her twenty-eight-year-old daughter,
Paula, to porphyria. Paula lingered in a coma for six months before dying. For

three years, Isabel saw the world in shades of gray. When she finally began to see color again, Isabel had a dream:

> [Paula] began to rise, and I with her, clinging to the cloth of her dress . . . We flew over valleys and hills, and finally descended into a forest of ancient redwoods . . . Paula pointed to the stream; I saw fresh roses lying along its banks . . . I felt myself sinking into that cool water, and knew that the voyage through pain was ending in an absolute void. As I dissolved, I had the revelation that the void was filled with everything the universe holds . . . Sacramental light and unfathomable darkness. I am the void, I am everything that exists . . . I am Paula and I am also Isabel, I am nothing and all other things in this life and other lives, immortal.
>
> Godspeed, Paula, woman.
> Welcome, Paula, spirit.

Time passed and Isabel continued to mourn. Then she began to notice the life around her. Finally, she was reunited with the part of herself that was missing, and she was renewed. It seems that only by letting go of the world as we expect it to be can we grow into spiritual fullness.

Demeter, by using her power to get her daughter back, teaches women that they do not always have to submit to others' decisions, and shows them that they have the authority to change the course of events. In Aristophanes's play *Lysistrata,* the women of Greece withhold sexual pleasures from men as a way of forcing the men to stop a war. We, too, must claim our power and use it constructively. We are the healers, caretakers, and mothers of our world.

When Demeter got Persephone back, they were both changed. Because they experienced life without each other and faced the possibility that they might never see each other again, they perceived things in a new light. Out of that transformation, the Eleusinian Mysteries were born. They were central to the religion of the ancient Greeks. People of all classes—from the ruling elite to their slaves—were allowed to participate in the mysteries. The initiates wore laurel wreaths as they walked a sacred road and crossed a narrow bridge before entering the hall of rituals in Demeter's temple. There, they chanted and danced in honor of the two goddesses and celebrated the return of Kore. Through sound, movement, and fasting, the initiates would reenact and symbolically experience the three phases of the myth—innocence, loss, and reunion. They learned how to evoke mystical states of consciousness under the protection of vigilant priests, called hierophants, who helped them purify their souls. Those who experienced the Eleusinian Mysteries overcame their fear of death, having learned that there is an afterlife. The initiates ultimately gained a sense of freedom when they discovered that earthly existence is not the only reality. That was the sacred gift of the Eleusinian Mysteries: the death of the worldly self and the rebirth of a person's divine essence.

> VERILY, VERILY, I SAY UNTO YOU, EXCEPT A CORN OF
> WHEAT FALL INTO THE GROUND AND DIE, IT ABIDETH
> ALONE; BUT IF IT DIE, IT BRINGETH FORTH MUCH FRUIT.
> —*John* 12:24–5

In Demeter's strong longing to reunite with her lost child, we see our own strong desire to reunite with the lost child within, the lost maiden that Carl Jung calls the anima. When we cling too strongly to our attachments in the external world, we suffer and grieve, very much like Demeter when she lost Persephone. Just as the seasons change, our physical, emotional, and spiritual selves go through similar cycles. There is wisdom to be found when we understand these cycles, which can ultimately lead to the union of our earthly and spiritual beings.

How to Get in Touch with Demeter

Nurture Yourself and Others

✦ Learn to mother yourself. Spend time listening to your thoughts and feelings; notice ways in which you can better care for yourself. Your eating habits, the way you dress, and your physical health all deserve the attention of kind Demeter. Replace your harsh, self-critical inner voice with loving words and nurturing thoughts.

✦ Prepare an abundant, nurturing meal—perhaps bake your own bread—and invite your friends to enjoy the fruits of your labors. Volunteer to serve at a homeless shelter. Feeding the hungry can satisfy our desire to nurture and to serve.

✦ If you don't have children and want an outlet for your mothering instincts, spend time with your friends' children. Visit an orphanage or foundling hospital. Hold babies and give them the nurturing they need and deserve.

Enhance Your Relationship with Your Mother

✦ Write a letter to your mother and thank her for all she did for you. Forgive her for things you think she should have done differently. Allow compassion for her humanness to fill your heart.

✦ Visualize your mother standing in front of you. Between the two of you, see an umbilical cord. With a large pair of imaginary scissors, which you see in your hand, cut the cord. Put the scissors down. Wrap the end of the cord up into your navel, sealing it in. With your eyes closed, place both hands on your heart. Look again at your mother. You may be holding back deep feelings and emotions that need to come to the surface. Take some very deep breaths. Take the time to really experience this; do not rush. Allow this to happen. If you need to say something aloud to your mother (or to yourself), do so. Now visualize a thick umbilical cord extending from your heart all the way up through the top of your head, connecting you to your spirit. Let the energy embrace you. Be receptive to the love that is available for you from your soul. It waits for you, and it can help you to achieve greater freedom and self-confidence. (A suggestion: record the steps to this visualization exercise on tape.)

Connect with Mother Earth

✦ Spend time on a farm, where you can learn age-old ways of relating to animals and to the land itself.

✦ Volunteer in a park or garden, where you can tend plants closely, watching them grow, and thus help bring beauty into your community. Create a garden at home.

✦ Walk barefoot on the earth.

A LITERARY REFLECTION
DEMETER

"SIR,

"YOU ASK ME TO COME SPEND A WEEK WITH YOU, WHICH MEANS I WOULD BE NEAR MY DAUGHTER, WHOM I ADORE. YOU WHO LIVE WITH HER KNOW HOW RARELY I SEE HER, HOW MUCH HER PRESENCE DELIGHTS ME, AND I'M TOUCHED THAT YOU SHOULD ASK ME TO COME SEE HER. ALL THE SAME, I'M NOT GOING TO ACCEPT YOUR KIND INVITATION, FOR THE TIME BEING AT ANY RATE. THE REASON IS THAT MY PINK CACTUS IS PROBABLY GOING TO FLOWER. IT'S A VERY RARE PLANT I'VE BEEN GIVEN, AND I'M TOLD THAT IN OUR CLIMATE IT FLOWERS ONLY ONCE EVERY FOUR YEARS. NOW, I AM ALREADY A VERY OLD WOMAN, AND IF I WENT AWAY WHEN MY PINK CACTUS IS ABOUT TO FLOWER, I AM CERTAIN I SHOULDN'T SEE IT FLOWER AGAIN.

"SO I BEG YOU, SIR, TO ACCEPT MY SINCERE THANKS AND MY REGRETS, TOGETHER WITH MY KIND REGARDS."

THIS NOTE, SIGNED "SIDONIE COLETTE, NÉE LANDOY," WAS WRITTEN BY MY MOTHER TO ONE OF MY HUSBANDS, THE SECOND. A YEAR LATER SHE DIED, AT THE AGE OF SEVENTY-SEVEN.

WHENEVER I FEEL MYSELF INFERIOR TO EVERYTHING ABOUT ME, THREATENED BY MY OWN MEDIOCRITY, FRIGHTENED BY THE DISCOVERY THAT A MUSCLE IS LOSING ITS STRENGTH . . . I CAN STILL HOLD UP MY HEAD AND SAY TO MYSELF: "I AM THE DAUGHTER OF

THE WOMAN WHO WROTE THAT LETTER—THAT LETTER
AND SO MANY MORE THAT I HAVE KEPT. THIS ONE
TELLS ME IN TEN LINES THAT AT THE AGE OF SEVENTY-
SIX SHE WAS PLANNING JOURNEYS AND UNDERTAKING
THEM, BUT THAT WAITING FOR THE POSSIBLE BURSTING
INTO BLOOM OF A TROPICAL FLOWER HELD EVERY-
THING UP AND SILENCED EVEN HER HEART, MADE
FOR LOVE. I AM THE DAUGHTER OF A WOMAN WHO,
IN A MEAN, CLOSE-FISTED, CONFINED LITTLE PLACE,
OPENED HER VILLAGE HOME TO STRAY CATS, TRAMPS
AND PREGNANT SERVANT-GIRLS. I AM THE DAUGHTER
OF A WOMAN WHO MANY A TIME, WHEN SHE WAS IN
DESPAIR AT NOT HAVING ENOUGH MONEY FOR OTHERS,
RAN THROUGH THE WIND-WHIPPED SNOW TO CRY
FROM DOOR TO DOOR, AT THE HOUSES OF THE RICH,
THAT A CHILD HAD JUST BEEN BORN IN A POVERTY-
STRICKEN HOME TO PARENTS WHOSE FEEBLE, EMPTY
HANDS HAD NO SWADDLING CLOTHES FOR IT. LET ME
NOT FORGET THAT I AM THE DAUGHTER OF A WOMAN
WHO BENT HER HEAD, TREMBLING, BETWEEN THE
BLADES OF A CACTUS, HER WRINKLED FACE FULL OF
ECSTASY OVER THE PROMISE OF A FLOWER, A WOMAN
WHO HERSELF NEVER CEASED TO FLOWER, UNTIRINGLY,
DURING THREE-QUARTERS OF A CENTURY.

—Colette, *Break of Day*

HERA

GODDESS OF MARRIAGE

THE MYTH

BORN OF CRONUS AND RHEA ON THE ISLAND OF SAMOS, Hera is the queen of Olympus and the goddess of marriage. She is also both the wife and the twin sister of Zeus, the king of the gods. In the *Iliad*, Homer calls her "Queen of Heaven" and "Hera of the Golden Throne." She is also called the white-armed goddess, a romantic image that evokes moonbeams spreading throughout the night sky. Her name is thought by some people to be an ancient Greek word meaning "lady." After she was born, the Seasons were her nurses; hence, she is goddess of the calendar year, and is frequently pictured with a cuckoo on her scepter, symbolizing spring, and autumn's ripe pomegranate in her left hand, symbolizing the death of the year.

After banishing their father, Cronus, Zeus courted Hera in Knossos, on the island of Crete, where his initial efforts proved fruitless. Hera remained unmoved despite Zeus's pleas. Finally, in the midst of a raging storm, Zeus disguised himself as a cuckoo, wet, shivering, and frightened, and it was then that Hera at last took pity on him, tenderly warming him in her bosom. As soon as he attained that coveted spot, Zeus resumed his true, glorious, magnificent form and ravished her. Ashamed by what happened, Hera agreed to marry Zeus, but throughout their marriage she constantly reminded him of her former independence and how he had tricked her into marriage.

The royal couple's wedding on Mount Olympus was a glorious celebration, to which all the gods brought gifts. The wedding night, on the island of Samos, lasted three hundred years. Theirs was called the *hieros gamos* (sacred marriage), which is celebrated in many cultures as the union of the earth goddess and the sky god, who regenerate the cosmos with their lovemaking.

Hera and Zeus had two sons—Ares (god of war) and Hephaestus (god of fire)—and a daughter, Hebe. Hephaestus, the blacksmith of the gods, is sometimes said to have been born out of Hera's thigh. He became a master craftsman, and invented a chair with a manacling device, which he once used to trap Hera until she revealed the secret of his birth. Although Hephaestus had become lame when Zeus threw him off Olympus for taking Hera's side against him, she never showed very much affection toward her son.

In fact, Hera rarely showed affection for any members of her family. Most of the time, she remained bitter and frustrated by Zeus's unbounded promiscuity. Their quarrels, and Hera's acts of revenge, were notorious on Olympus. Two of her favorite techniques for punishing Zeus were the banishment of all his children conceived with other women and the transformation of his lovers into beasts. In one instance, she turned Io into a cow, but when Zeus continued to love her, Hera had her driven out of Greece into Egypt by a gadfly. On another occasion, she sent two snakes into the cradle of baby Hercules, the son of Zeus and Alcmene, but Hercules strangled the snakes and escaped. Later in his life, Hera drove Hercules to murder his wife and children in a fit of madness. Even after that, Hera persisted in her persecution of Hercules, helping Eurystheus, king of Mycenae, to devise a series of twelve backbreaking labors for Hercules to perform as "penance." It was only after Hercules became deified that he and Hera were reconciled and she gave him her daughter, Hebe, in marriage. Thereafter, Hera loved him as a son.

The list of Hera's vengeful deeds is endless: in one famous story, she sent monsters to chase Leto, whom Zeus (in the guise of a swan) seduced and impregnated, from island to island and country to country to prevent her from giving birth to Apollo and his twin sister, Artemis. She had Semele burned alive; when Athamas and Ino helped rear Semele's orphaned son, Dionysus, she rained calamities down upon them. After Zeus changed Callisto into a bear, Hera had Artemis shoot it. She kidnapped Lamia's children, causing the distraught mother to become a compulsive kidnapper. But Zeus could be jealous, too. Many who lusted after Hera received treatment similar to that which befell Zeus's paramours. Endymion may have been sent into his eternal sleep because of a dalliance with her. Ixion fell in love with her, but ejaculated into a phantom cloud resembling Hera that was created by Zeus. By this phantom, he became the father of the Centaurs.

Hera can also be extraordinarily vain. Not surprisingly, the peacock is one of her symbols. Whenever a mortal presumes to set her beauty above Hera's, the result is predictable. Proetus's three daughters were said to have been driven mad by Hera as punishment for making this comparison. Side, the wife of Orion, was sent immediately to Hades for a similar offense. Rhodope and her husband, Haemus, were so happy that they compared their estate with that of Zeus and Hera, and for this offense they were changed into mountains.

Hera is also said to have been consumed by her sexuality. She often borrowed Aphrodite's girdle to guarantee her attractiveness to her husband, and she went to the spring of Canathus every year to renew her virginity. Once, it is said, Zeus and Hera argued about whether men or women derived more pleasure from the sexual act. Hera maintained that men did, in view of their infidelity and promiscuity. Zeus maintained that women did, citing Hera's own enjoyment of lovemaking as proof. They sought out Tiresias to give them the answer. Having been both a man and a woman, Tiresias was in a position to know. Without hesitation, Tiresias answered that women receive nine times the pleasure: "If the parts of love-pleasure be counted as ten, thrice three go to women, one only to men." Hera reacted by striking him blind.

There is a beautiful story about the goddess that shows a different side to her. When she could no longer put up with Zeus's infidelities, she left him and returned to her birthplace. To persuade her to come back to him, Zeus approached the mountain Cithaeron with a veiled female statue, which he said was a local princess who had agreed to become his bride. Hera discovered the deceit and smiled. Filled with an inner wisdom that left no room for raging or jealousy, she did indeed reconcile with him. From that moment forward, something was radically different between them. By distancing herself, Hera had reconnected with her true power. At that point, she was ready for the marriage for which she had longed, because she was finally independent from him and had accepted him for who he was. She would no longer be controlled by him. That was her freedom.

Despite her unattractive characteristics, the worship of Hera was widespread and intense, partly because she was able to give humans the gift of prophecy, a talent revered by the Greeks. She was known as Hera Parthenos (maiden), Hera Teleia (fully grown, complete), and Hera Chera (widow). These three aspects of her personality were identified by the Greeks with the three stages of the moon—the waxing moon was Hera the maiden, the full moon was Hera the fulfilled wife, and the waning moon was Hera as an abandoned, withdrawn woman. The Orphic hymn to Hera invokes her thus:

> You are ensconced in darksome hollows, and
>   airy is your form,
> O Hera, queen of all the blessed consorts of
>   Zeus.
> You send soft breezes to mortals, such as nourish
>   the soul,
> and, O mother of rains, you nurture the
>   winds and give birth to all.
> Without you there is neither life nor growth:
> and, mixed as you are in the air we venerate,
>   you partake of all,
> and of all you are queen and mistress.
> You toss and turn with the rushing wind.
> May you, O blessed goddess and many-named
>   queen of all,
> come with kindness and joy on your lovely
>   face.

THE SYMBOLS

PEACOCK
This bird, with its lavish display of tail feathers, symbolizes pride, vanity, and royalty.

THRONE OF GOLD AND IVORY
This royal throne is a fitting symbol of Hera's power over gods and mortals, and of the stateliness that comes with her position.

CUCKOO

The loud, monotonous call of this bird is often associated with an augury of the future. Hera has the power to confer the gift of prophecy on man or beast.

TEMPLE

The temple is where the realm of heaven and the realm of earth meet. As such, it not only symbolizes the divine but also the various sacraments, like marriage, that take place in it.

Two golden rings

Two rings joined
together stand for
permanence, partnership,
and strength in unity.

Wind

Because of its seeming
randomness and
unpredictability, wind
is an ancient symbol of
divine will. Wind can also
symbolize outrage, and the
power to destroy anything
in its path.

THE ARCHETYPE
THE POWER OF PARTNERSHIP

ERA, AS THE GODDESS OF MARRIAGE, REPRESENTS the commitment between husband and wife. She endures the challenges of matrimony despite its intense difficulties. Powerful, beautiful, regal, and proud, she can also be bitter, quarrelsome, jealous, and possessive. These negative qualities can be partially explained by her husband's infidelity and his feeling of entitlement toward his extramarital exploits.

Contemporary women who possess Hera's positive qualities identify themselves as wives with no sense of frustration or resentment. They are equal partners with their husbands. They are confident and have no trouble asserting their authority in and out of the relationship. They are often pillars of their community and make a significant impact on society.

Women who embody Hera's power wisely choose men who are secure in themselves and who don't feel threatened by their wives. These women are supportive of and protective of their husbands' endeavors, and make sure that all their husbands' needs are met. They understand the potential for creating a wonderful, powerful, potent union in which women can be fulfilled through their husbands and vice versa.

Society draws on the continuous exuberance of the Hera woman and her seemingly boundless supply of time and energy. If you are manifesting that aspect of Hera, you are probably using your husband's power, position, and money to contribute to charities, churches, schools, and hospitals. Most first ladies exemplify the archetypal Hera. According to Judy Chicago, writing in *The Dinner Party*, Abigail Adams, the wife of President John Adams and mother of President John Quincy Adams, was "a patriot, revolutionary, abolitionist, writer and feminist. She managed all the business and farm affairs for her family, advised her husband, John, and was one of the great letter writers of her time. She spoke out against slavery eighty-five years before the abolitionist movement." Queen Victoria—who reigned over Great Britain and Ireland, married her first cousin, Prince Albert, and bore him nine children—was the namesake for an entire movement in Western cultural and political history. Empress Theodora—an extraordinary woman known both as an actress and as a prostitute—married the emperor Justinian and became the empress of the Eastern Roman Empire. She made tremendous contributions to political and religious policy, and brought about a lot of reforms for the benefit of women—making rape a capital crime, allowing women to inherit property, and punishing those who forced women to become prostitutes. She is known among historians as a better ruler than her husband.

On the positive side, Zeus and Hera represent the ultimate union of male and female. Theirs is a union of strength, like that of a king and a queen. It is a marriage of two people with healthy egos who know how to exercise their power. It is not a union formed for the sake of children or based on Eros, like the union of Aphrodite and Ares. The union of Zeus and Hera is cosmic, with transcendental moments—like their three-hundred-year wedding night. For them, the institution of marriage comes first.

Following the positive example of Zeus and Hera, the best marriages I've seen unite two people who are focused on spiritual ideals; something bigger or more profound exists within them, bypassing the conflict of egos and personalities. Joseph Campbell, in *The Power of Myth*, explains: "What is marriage? . . . It's the reunion of the separated duad. Originally you were one. You are now two in the world, but the recognition of the spiritual identity is what marriage is. It's different from a love affair. It has nothing to do with that. It's another mythological plane of experience. When people get married because they think it's a long-time love affair, they'll be divorced very soon, because all love affairs end in disappointment. But marriage is recognition of a spiritual identity. If we live a proper life, if our minds are on the right qualities in regarding the person of the opposite sex, we will find our proper male or female counterpart. But if we are distracted by certain sensuous interests, we'll marry the wrong person. By marrying the right person, we reconstruct the image of the incarnate God, and that's what marriage is. . . . Marriage is not a simple love affair, it's an ordeal, and the ordeal is the sacrifice of ego to a relationship in which two have become one."

The word "ordeal" is indeed an accurate description of Hera's marriage to Zeus. Just like some modern wives, she ends up betrayed and dishonored, disregarded by her husband. She has to witness not only his numerous love affairs but also the births of his numerous illegitimate children, and she is powerless to do anything about it. That powerlessness can bring out the darkest, most negative aspect of ourselves. When confronted with it, we will either collapse into depression or become consumed with rage, jealousy, and vengefulness. It is often what happens to women who are creatively unfulfilled, who do not realize that a strong union results from two people who are strong and complete as individuals. By neglecting herself, a woman can become bitter, a hag, a nag, a shrew—the very image of clinging possessiveness, like Martha in Edward Albee's *Who's Afraid of Virginia Woolf?* I have met many women who are in a permanent state of war with their husbands; the worst part of it is they are so stuck in their web that they see no way out and are filled with the fear of being left alone. As Sally, a frustrated wife, in Sally Kempton's article "Cutting Loose" says:

> I used to lie in bed beside my husband and wish I had the courage to bash in his head with a frying pan. I would do it while he slept, since awake he would overpower me, disarm me. If I only dared, I would mutter to myself through clenched teeth, pushing back the realization that I didn't dare, not because I was afraid of seriously hurting him—I would have loved to do that—but because even in the extremity of my anger I was afraid that if I cracked his head with a frying pan, he would leave me.

Often, women who give up everything for a man—leave their families, deny their values, and make him the center of their lives—do not have a strong sense of self. If the man they have given up so much for should leave, these women can become obsessed with destroying the "other woman," or will constantly look for ways to punish the man.

Medea, the main character in Euripides's play of the same name, is perhaps

the most extreme example of the betrayed wife. She is a sorceress, the beautiful, exotic daughter of Aeetes, king of Colchis, who holds the golden fleece in his possession. Jason and the Argonauts want to steal the fleece and bring it back to Greece. Through the intervention of Aphrodite, Medea falls in love with Jason; he promises to marry her if she will use her powers to help him steal the fleece. She does—so devoted to Jason that she kills her own brother in the process— and she and Jason marry. They move to Corinth and have two sons. Jason, unhappy in his marriage to Medea, seizes the opportunity to marry the daughter of Creon, the king of Corinth, and sends Medea and their children into exile so he will be free to remarry. Medea feels completely discounted, humiliated, and betrayed. She gives Creon's daughter a dress as a wedding present, which bursts into flames as soon as she puts it on, killing her instantly. Immediately afterward, she kills her two children, thus inflicting upon Jason the cruelest possible revenge. She then disappears, leaving him bereft and alone.

Society has definitely impressed upon women the necessity for marriage. In Greece, when a woman finishes college, she is expected to marry. For me, marriage and the Hera archetype were very much in the background. I did not feel the pull of Hera but rather that of Artemis or Athena—the urge to be independent and create my own identity through work and personal growth. The hardest part was overcoming the societal conditioning that I couldn't be completely validated as a woman unless I were married. I wasn't even conscious of being influenced by that belief until I found all my friends setting me up to get married. When I realized that marriage was not my primary focus, and claimed my own truth, I relaxed and became very happy; no Heras were pressuring me anymore. It was a great liberation to realize that my value and confidence as a woman doesn't come from a man loving me and attending to me. My fulfillment lies within myself.

Carl Jung believed that in order for human beings to be whole we have to integrate the male and female aspects of ourselves, so that when we are attracted to someone we recognize our own characteristics in him or her. In marriage, we are committing to the revelation of the most elemental aspects of ourselves, which are sometimes dark, vulnerable, and wounded. When Hera is betrayed, these aspects—rage, anger, and jealousy—come to the fore.

Nature has powerful, uncanny ways to pull us toward the integration of our male and female qualities. Joseph Campbell says that we know we have chosen the right person when we feel this integration instinctively: "Your heart tells you. It ought to. . . . That's the mystery . . . but there's a flash that comes, and something in you knows that this is the one."

Often, a young Hera will experience a tremendous urge to be married; she wants that ring on her finger, the symbol of union. When she is with her boyfriend, she already looks married, she already treats him as a husband— unlike the Aphrodite woman, who is always flirting and enticing, courting and romancing. A Hera woman's wedding day is the most important day in her life. It is then that she assumes the role of wife: she gives up her old identity and takes her husband's name. If she's chosen wisely and her husband honors the marriage as much as she does, and if he is devoted to her and appreciates her, she is fulfilled. However, if she has chosen a husband whose attention is on his work and other activities, who ignores her and takes her for granted, she and her marriage will suffer. She will have to concentrate on her own growth and discover an identity independent of him.

Federico Fellini created a movie called *Juliet of the Spirits* about a proper and virtuous housewife who discovers that her beloved husband is having a secret love affair. Said Fellini of his goals in making the film: "I want to help Italian women become free of a certain kind of conditioning produced by the middle-class marriage. They are so full of fear. They are so full of idealism. I want them to try to understand that they are alone, and that this is not a bad thing. To be alone is to be all of yourself. Italian women have this myth of the husband. I want to show that it is sentimental, this myth. . . . The intention of the film is to restore woman to her true independence, her indisputable and inalienable dignity . . . The wife must not be the Madonna, nor an instrument of pleasure, and least of all a servant."

When a woman decides to take her power back from a marriage that isn't working or isn't fulfilling to her, this is the first stage in the process of reclaiming herself. Her inner Hera can be a most invaluable guide at this point. For example, when Hera became fed up with Zeus's infidelities and her own feelings of powerlessness, she returned to her homeland. There, she spent time in solitude.

She distanced herself from the relationship in order to heal, and it was only then that she was able to meet her husband again—as if for the first time—not in need, but in fullness. If you are in that stage of your journey, you need to reestablish your relationship with yourself, so that you can either leave the marriage or return to it intact—a kind of Hera Teleia, fully grown and complete. It is Hera Teleia who is ready for the ideal marriage she envisions. Kahlil Gibran speaks beautifully about this kind of partnership:

> YOU WERE BORN TOGETHER, AND TOGETHER YOU
> SHALL BE FOREVERMORE . . .
> BUT LET THERE BE SPACES IN YOUR TOGETHERNESS,
> AND LET THE WINDS OF THE HEAVENS DANCE
> BETWEEN YOU.
>
> LOVE ONE ANOTHER BUT MAKE NOT A BOND OF LOVE:
> LET IT RATHER BE A MOVING SEA BETWEEN THE
> SHORES OF YOUR SOULS.
> FILL EACH OTHER'S CUP BUT DRINK NOT FROM ONE
> CUP . . .
> SING AND DANCE TOGETHER AND BE JOYOUS, BUT LET
> EACH ONE OF YOU BE ALONE . . .
> AND STAND TOGETHER YET NOT TOO NEAR TOGETHER:
> FOR THE PILLARS OF THE TEMPLE STAND APART,
> AND THE OAK TREE AND THE CYPRESS GROW NOT IN
> EACH OTHER'S SHADOW.

Take Command of Yourself and Renew Your Environment

✦ Practice the following visualization exercise. Close your eyes and imagine taking a few steps into a magnificent temple. As you enter it, you are enveloped by a warm purple light. In the center you see a beautiful throne. Sit on it and make yourself comfortable. Take a few deep breaths, exhaling any inner tension, and then relax. The solid foundation of the temple, its protective roof, and the immense power of its columns evoke a feeling of strength inside you. Reflect upon your life. See if there are any areas that you would like to strengthen—your willpower, your body, your personal and professional relationships. Say out loud to yourself, "I now take responsibility over all aspects of my life. No matter what the circumstances, I reign supreme over myself." Think of specific actions you can take to feel empowered and secure. As you get ready to leave the temple, take a moment to stand tall. Take a deep breath, revitalizing yourself with a new feeling of authority. As you open your eyes, remind yourself that you have the power to choose your thoughts, feelings, and actions to bring about the positive changes you desire. (A suggestion: record the steps to this visualization exercise on tape.)

✦ Create a home that energizes you. Clear out the clutter. Revitalize the decor with plants, new colors, softer lights, or new window treatments. Ask a friend with a good sense of style for advice if you need support.

Strengthen Your Partnerships

✦ Be a mediator: if you are around friends or colleagues who are disagreeing, be supportive if asked. Help them find solutions that will disarm the negative situation.

✦ If you already enjoy a loving relationship and want to reinvigorate it, renew your vows in a ceremony of your own design that you can hold in the intimacy of your own home. No clergyman is necessary; create a sacred environment, invite a few friends, and recommit to each other.

✦ Step forward and hold that scepter high. Be a leader; serve your community; make a difference in the lives of others. You must be heard and must be seen.

✦ Host an event that will bring people together who would enjoy and benefit from each other's company.

Identify Your Needs

✦ If you are an unmarried Hera looking for your spouse, be very clear about the qualities you want in a partner and in your relationship. Write down all the doubts you have about achieving your ideal, then burn the paper. You created those doubts; now you can destroy them.

✦ Become aware of what you need from your partner. Openly discuss your needs and listen to his needs as well.

✦ Watch the movie *Shirley Valentine*, directed by Lewis Gilbert, the story of a frustrated housewife in Liverpool who goes for a Greek vacation and . . . just watch it and see what happens!

A Literary Reflection

Within the bond of marriage, tell me, Brutus,
is it excepted I should know no secrets
That appertain to you? Am I yourself
But, as it were, in sort or limitation,—
To keep with you at meals, comfort your bed,
And talk to you sometimes? Dwell I but
   in the suburbs
Of your good pleasure? If it be no more,
Portia is Brutus' harlot, not his wife . . .
I grant I am a woman; but withal
A woman that Lord Brutus took to wife:
I grant I am a woman; but withal
A woman well-reputed,—Cato's daughter.
Think you I am no stronger than my sex,
Being so father'd and so husbanded?
Tell me your counsels, I will not disclose 'em:
I have made strong proof of my constancy,
Giving myself a voluntary wound
Here in the thigh: can I bear that with patience,
And not my husband's secrets?

—Portia, the wife of Brutus, in Shakespeare's *Julius Caesar*

HESTIA
Goddess of the Hearth and Home

THE MYTH

ESTİA, THE OLDEST DAUGHTER OF THE TİTAnS Cronus and Rhea, is the sister of Zeus, king of the gods, and of Poseidon, king of the sea. Robert Graves calls her the "mildest, most upright, and most charitable of all the Olympians." Hestia is not only the goddess of the hearth and domestic life, she is, more specifically (and more importantly), the goddess of the fire that burns within the hearth. This fire symbolizes the inner light that burns within each of us, recharging and rekindling our spirits. In ancient Greece, the domestic hearth was regarded as a sacrificial altar to Hestia, and represented personal security, happiness, and the sacred duty of hospitality. It is Hestia's warm and holy presence that transforms a house into a home. Hestia is also credited with the invention of domestic architecture, which in ancient times featured the hearth at the exact physical center of the house. Homes were literally constructed outward, after the hearth was in place, symbolizing the orientation of the family—and the soul—around its essential core.

The idea of the hearth, a perpetual flame representing the center of one's orderly life, extended beyond the sphere of the home to include public life as well. Ancient Greeks considered domestic life subordinate to the life of the state, and they honored Hestia not only as the center of the house but as the center of the city and even the world. Each Greek metropolis had a public hearth in the center of town, called a *prytaneion*, where ambassadors and other visitors were received and where suppliants could find asylum. In addition, when citizens wanted to found a new colony in another city, they carried the fire from this public hearth with them and used it to establish a public hearth in the new place. If the flame of any public hearth ever went out, it had to be started again from scratch, not from a preexisting flame. Throughout the centuries, the flame of the Olympic torch has been carried as a reminder of Hestia's importance.

There are no statues of Hestia because she is an essence rather than a form.

Wherever there is a fire lit in her honor, invoking her presence, there is her temple. In Delphi, she had her own place of worship called the *omphalos* (the Greek word for "navel"), where a fire continuously burned. In Rome, Hestia was called Vesta and she was worshiped at the public hearth in the center of the city. This hearth was established to guarantee Rome's historical permanence, and was attended to by six virgin priestesses known as the Vestal Virgins. The English words "vest" and "investment" derive from the goddess's name, connoting protection and security. The Romans also believed that Vesta presided over the preparation of meals, and so the first mouthful of food was always consecrated to her at the ritual beginning of every meal.

Hestia is one of the three virgin goddesses of Olympus, the other two being Artemis and Athena. Hestia vowed to her brother Zeus that she would remain a virgin forever in a symbolic gesture of spiritual purity and integrity. Even Aphrodite could not entice Hestia to any amorous feelings: both her brother Poseidon and her nephew Apollo wanted to marry her, but she resisted. She even fought off Priapus, a demigod who symbolizes fertility, when he tried to rape her at a rustic feast.

There are very few stories about Hestia in mythological literature. She does not figure in any of the Homeric hymns or epics, and she—perhaps alone among all the Olympians—does not enter into any disputes with her fellow deities. Her power is in her being—she does not strive or seek to accomplish. There are no quarrels, competitions, lovers, conquests, adventures, or romances. She remains centered, refusing to compromise. Her name, according to Plato, means "the essence of things," and this makes her perhaps the most ethereal, the least personal of all the goddesses. Even two-dimensional images of her usually portray her as veiled, calm and dignified, and unyielding. She is at once imposing and discreet, and far less dramatic than the other goddesses. Her place at the center of everything ties her with notions of centricity in the earth and even in the universe, and gives her some of the attributes of the goddesses of the earth and the underworld, like Cybele (often identified with Rhea), Gaia (Mother Earth), Demeter, and Persephone. Nevertheless, Hestia remains a distinct personality—stately, distant, but ever faithful, ever bright, and ever warming.

THE SYMBOLS

FLAMING HEARTH

Wherever there is a flaming hearth, the presence of Hestia can be felt. It is a symbol of warmth, security, and domestic tranquility.

GLOBE

The roundness of this icon symbolizes Hestia's presence at the center of things; it can also mean universal acceptance and constancy regardless of location.

ALTAR

The altar represents sacredness as well as a silent presence, the spiritual core within us all.

VEST

The vest is a symbol of protection, comfort, and even modesty.

LOCKED BOX

The locked box is both a symbol of virginity and a symbol of safety. The box is the repository of the treasures of the home and of the self. The lock means these treasures are well guarded and that the box is protected.

SHELTER

The shelter represents Hestia's protective qualities. In this goddess's presence, we feel at home with ourselves.

THE ARCHETYPE
THE POWER OF BEING CENTERED

WHENEVER I GIVE A TALK ABOUT GODDESSES, I'm always amazed at the fact that everybody seems to have heard of Aphrodite, Athena, and the other goddesses I discuss, but almost no one remembers Hestia. Her gifts are hidden in the inner, quiet corners of ourselves. It's no surprise that in our busy world, filled with activities and external stimulation, we have lost sight of the fact that there is a force larger than ourselves that sustains us. In order to bring Hestia more into our lives, we have to do one of the hardest things that will ever be asked of us—nothing.

Joseph Campbell, in *The Power of Myth*, writes of the human need to have a sacred place where temporal walls can dissolve and where wonderment can flourish: "You must have a room, or a certain hour or so a day, where you don't know what was in the newspapers that morning, you don't know who your friends are, you don't know what you owe anybody, you don't know what anybody owes to you. This is a place where you can simply experience and bring forth what you are and what you might be. This is the place of creative incubation. At first you may find that nothing happens there. But if you have a sacred place and use it, something eventually will happen. . . . Where is your bliss station? You have to try to find it."

The woman who exemplifies the qualities of Hestia understands, more than any other goddess, the value of such a place.

The Hestia woman experiences tremendous peace and joy just from being in her home. Housework is not unpleasant for her; it's an expression of the harmony she feels inside. She can be alone without being lonesome because she feels connected to everything outside of her. Home is her sanctuary; it reflects her soulfulness. The Hestia woman doesn't crave attention; she may appear simple and ordinary. She can easily be overlooked. A world that glorifies physical beauty and competition can, unfortunately, discount the grace and richness of the Hestia woman. She intuitively knows that the meaning of her life springs from

116

her spiritual center, and brings with her a sense of security that is more priceless than the most lavish material possessions.

Hestia teaches us that we can be at home with ourselves wherever we are, no matter whom we are with. When we are unaware of Hestia's influence, we feel as though something is amiss—we feel disconnected, off-center, anxious, and discontent. Our soul has no resting place, and our minds are filled with distractions. Hestia provides us with a structure that protects us from the invasion of the outside world, which is essential to keep our internal flame burning.

Hestia nurtures everyone who dwells within the sanctuary of the hearth; her unconditional love does not discriminate. Sometimes this extends beyond the genetic, nuclear family to the "family of man." Elsa Gidlow, in her poem "Chains of Fire," evokes the influence of Hestia across races and cultures:

> Touching the match, waiting for creeping flame,
> I know myself linked by chains of fires
> To every woman who has kept a hearth . . .
> I see mothers, grandmothers back to beginnings,
> Huddled beside holes in the earth . . .
> Guarding the magic no other being has learned,
> Awed, reverent, before the sacred fire
> Sharing live coals with the tribe.

Mother Teresa, more than anyone in modern times, exemplifies the Hestia archetype. This saintly woman practiced daily communion with the divine, through meditation and service to others. She was a living flame to many, always carrying a silence inside her. As she wrote in her book *In the Heart of the World:*

> We too are called to withdraw at certain intervals into deeper silence and aloneness with God, together as a community as well as personally. To be alone with him—not with our books, thoughts, and memories but completely stripped of everything—to dwell lovingly in his presence, silent, empty, expectant, and motionless. We cannot find God in noise or

AGITATION . . . IN SILENCE WE WILL FIND NEW ENERGY
AND TRUE UNITY. SILENCE GIVES US A NEW OUTLOOK
ON EVERYTHING.

Bringing Hestia into our lives transforms the mundane into the sacred, and our very homes become temples. All our activities become fulfilling, from washing dishes to creating art. Hestia's presence illuminates our existence, and allows us to walk in radiance. In the words of the poet Rainer Maria Rilke:

> A BILLION STARS GO SPINNING THROUGH THE NIGHT,
> BLAZING HIGH ABOVE YOUR HEAD.
> BUT IN YOU IS THE PRESENCE THAT WILL BE,
> WHEN THE STARS ARE DEAD.

How to Get in Touch with Hestia

 ## Sanctify Your Home

✦ Eliminate clutter from every room of your home. Keep those objects that support your sense of peace and discard those that disturb you.

✦ Create a sacred spot in a corner of your living room or bedroom. Make this spot your personal haven: fill it with candles, some flowers, incense, scented oils, and pictures that evoke the divine.

✦ Keep a candle or two burning when you are at home in honor of the sacred flame that is always burning inside you.

 ## Sanctify Your Daily Life

✦ Whenever you can, get together with a group of friends around a fireplace. If you can, build a campfire outdoors and enjoy each other's company.

✦ Find a place outside your home—for example, a garden—where you can "get away from it all." Visit it often. Allow its stillness and calmness to guide you to your inner self.

◆ Spend a little time before you start the day's activities, with the following visualization exercise. Close your eyes, take a deep breath, exhale, and relax your body. Imagine the tiles and stones of a hearth around you. Inside your heart, visualize a flame that burns any anxieties, preoccupations, or negative feelings into ash. Let that flame warm you and its heat envelop you until you become completely present and still in the center of that hearth. From the bottom of your feet to the top of your head, breathe in the warmth and protection and sense of security until you become one with it. Open your eyes and go about your daily activities. Find a moment during the day when you can rekindle that flame. (A suggestion: record the steps to this visualization exercise on tape.)

◆ Write a letter to yourself describing what your life would be like if you lived it from your center.

A Literary Reflection

Hestia

Love all Creation
The whole of it and every grain of sand
Love every leaf
Every ray of God's light
Love the animals
Love the plants
Love everything
If you love everything
You will perceive
The divine mystery in things
And once you have perceived it
You will begin to comprehend it ceaselessly
More and more everyday
And you will at last come to love the whole world
With an abiding universal love

—Fyodor Dostoyevsky

PERSEPHONE

GODDESS of DEATH, RENEWAL, and TRANSFORMATION

THE MYTH

ERSEPHONE IS THE BEAUTIFUL, INNOCENT YOUNG daughter of Zeus, king of the gods, and his sister, the goddess Demeter. Loved and adored by her mother, she is linked in every way with the Demeter myth. Her name derives from the Greek words *phero* and *phonos*, which mean together "she who brings destruction." She is also known as Kore, a Greek word for "daughter."

Persephone represents both light and darkness. The four stages of her life— her carefree and protected youth, her abduction and rape by Hades, her return to her mother and home, and her becoming queen of the underworld—reflect the alternating light and dark elements of all life on earth. Persephone shows us that we can grow and transform ourselves as we adapt to these experiences, steering us into awareness and wholeness.

The story of Persephone's abduction begins with Hades, king of the under-world, who for a long time had been asking his brother Zeus to help him find a wife. When Hades saw the young Persephone he fell in love with her, and asked Zeus to intercede with Persephone's mother, Demeter, on his behalf. Knowing Demeter would not want Persephone to become Hades's wife and therefore have to spend all her time underground, away from her, Zeus told Hades that the only way he could ever have Persephone all to himself was to kidnap her. Zeus and Hades contrived the perfect scheme. One day, Persephone was picking flowers when she came upon a narcissus, an intoxicatingly scented flower created by Gaia—Mother Earth, Persephone's grandmother—to lure her. As she reached for the hundred-petaled beauty, the earth suddenly opened beneath her, and Hades emerged in his golden chariot. Grabbing her, he plunged through the abyss and carried her into the underworld. Homer described the abduction in one of the earliest Homeric hymns:

> HE CAUGHT HOLD OF HER, PROTESTING, AND HE TOOK
> HER AWAY, WEEPING, IN HIS CHARIOT OF GOLD.

Then she screamed in a shrill voice, calling for her father, son of Chronos, the most powerful and best. But no one, not the immortal gods nor mortal men, no one heard her voice, not even the olive trees heavy with fruit.

The grief-stricken Demeter searched for her for nine days and nights without eating, drinking, or bathing, and finally threatened to bring famine to the earth, which would cause the destruction of all mankind. At last, Zeus relented and sent Hermes, the messenger of the gods, to tell Hades to return Persephone to her mother. Before he let her go, Hades persuaded his wife—who had eaten nothing in the underworld—to swallow a pomegranate seed. Unbeknownst to her, eating the food of the underworld meant that she was bound to return to the place, and so for all eternity, Persephone had to spend one-third of the year underground, with Hades, during which time Demeter caused the earth to lie bleak and barren. While she resided in Hades, Persephone served as queen of the underworld. She reigned over dead souls and guided the living who visited her realm. The other two-thirds of the year, when Persephone was with her mother, flowers, fruits, grains, and other crops could grow in profusion over the earth.

When Hades consummated his relationship with Persephone, he took her virginity. But because Hades was sterile, the couple could produce no offspring. However, Zeus found Persephone so attractive that he fathered several children by her, including Sabazius and Zagreus, said to be mystical incarnations of Dionysus. Apart from her interactions with Zeus, Persephone had a tranquil marriage with Hades and even grew to love him in her own way. When Hades had a clandestine affair with a nymph named Mintha, Persephone grew jealous and, with her mother's help, turned the nymph into a mint plant.

Persephone, on occasion, had physical desires unconnected with creating children. When Aphrodite left the baby Adonis, born to mortals from an incestuous relationship that she had brought about, in the care of Persephone in the underworld, Persephone became extremely fond of him. Years later, Aphrodite asked to have Adonis back, and Persephone refused to relinquish him. After all, he had grown into a breathtakingly handsome young man, and he and

Persephone had become lovers. To settle the dispute, Zeus decreed that Adonis would spend one-third of the year with Persephone, one-third with Aphrodite, and the remaining third alone to rest and recharge. Legend has it that eventually Adonis started to spend two-thirds of the year with Aphrodite, which made Persephone very jealous. When Adonis died (possibly from an attack by a boar), it was speculated that Persephone had engineered the fatal accident. Once Adonis was dead, Persephone could have him all to herself in the underworld. But it is in her role as Demeter's daughter, not Hades's wife, that Persephone was worshiped. She was the herald of spring, the reason Demeter awakened new life on earth every year. This powerful element of transformation remains central to the myth of Persephone and her importance to us today.

THE SYMBOLS

Narcissus

This sunny, fragrant flower symbolizes self-absorption. It is also a symbol of spring, when its conspicuous blossoms appear, as well as a symbol of death and rebirth.

Pomegranate

Because of its many seeds, this fruit symbolizes fertility. Hidden under the fruit's tough outer skin, the seeds symbolize the life of the emotions, hidden just under the surface.

Gates

However they are depicted, gates usually symbolize the entrance to another realm—the afterlife, the unconscious, or another domain of great power and significance.

Chariot

Many gods use a chariot as their mode of transportation between earth and their otherworldly palaces—in the case of Persephone, it symbolizes nothing less than the journey of transformation.

Two Faces

The penetrating gaze between the two faces symbolizes the bond between mother and daughter. Persephone and Demeter's relationship exemplifies this archetypical connection.

Spring

Persephone is the goddess of spring. This season of renewal is marked by the deity's ascension from Hades to Earth.

THE ARCHETYPE
THE POWER OF TRANSFORMATION

"WHO ARE YOU?" SAID THE CATERPILLAR.
THIS WAS NOT AN ENCOURAGING OPENING FOR A
CONVERSATION. ALICE REPLIED, RATHER SHYLY, "I—I
HARDLY KNOW, SIR, JUST AT PRESENT—AT LEAST I
KNOW WHO I WAS WHEN I GOT UP THIS MORNING, BUT
I THINK I MUST HAVE BEEN CHANGED SEVERAL TIMES
SINCE THEN."

"WHAT DO YOU MEAN BY THAT?" SAID THE
CATERPILLAR, STERNLY. "EXPLAIN YOURSELF!"

"I CAN'T EXPLAIN MYSELF, I'M AFRAID, SIR,"
SAID ALICE, "BECAUSE I'M NOT MYSELF, YOU SEE."

Alice, an innocent in Wonderland, might as well be speaking for Persephone, an innocent in the underworld, who, through her transformation from archetypal maiden into queen of the dead, bridges both the darkness and the light within. This integration occurs in four distinct phases: at first, Persephone is innocent and carefree; then her abduction and rape force her through a stage of loss and depression. In the third phase, Persephone reconnects with her mother as a woman, not as a child. Finally, she takes command of her own power, willingly returns to her husband, and becomes queen of the underworld, assisting others on their journey.

I have always felt a kinship with Persephone. Maybe this is because I was born on the first day of spring, and she is the goddess of spring. Maybe it's because my mother is an absolute archetypal mother just like Demeter, and I was so loved and cherished as a child. After this phase of innocence, I, too, experienced a dramatic loss: my parents' separation. My utopian reality collapsed, and I felt bereft, lonesome, and powerless; at the age of nine I had no voice to express my devastation. Although I moved with my mother and sister into a new, love-filled home, I missed my father terribly. I had virtually been abducted into a new

world, having had no choice in the matter. After I grew up, I remember a very distinct moment when I had a profound understanding that I exercised no control over other people's lives, including that of my parents. I knew I had finally integrated my parents' separation into the experience of my youth. When I understood the reason for my parents' decision, it helped me to see that there was one thing I could affect in my life: my own reactions. Like Persephone, I was empowered.

When Persephone plays in the meadows with the nymphs, secure and unselfconscious, basking in the rays of the sun and in her mother's all-encompassing, unconditional love, she is in the first phase of her journey—the phase of innocence. She is free, exploring the world with the uninhibited joy of a child. Jean Giraudoux describes this condition beautifully in *The Enchanted*:

> BETWEEN THE WORLD OF A YOUNG GIRL AND THE WORLD OF THE SPIRIT, THE WALL SEEMS NO MORE THAN A GOSSAMER; ONE WOULD SAY THAT AT ANY MOMENT, THROUGH THE SOUL OF A GIRL, THE INFINITE COULD FLOW INTO THE FINITE AND POSSESS IT UTTERLY.

At this stage of our lives, we are still unaware of our strengths. We rely on others for direction. Some women never outgrow this phase. They seem like adolescents, remaining uncommitted in every aspect of their lives.

In the second phase of her journey, Persephone, seduced by the intoxicating scent of the narcissus, reaches out to pick the flower. Suddenly the earth splits open and Hades snatches her. She is taken down to the underworld, through the abyss, and becomes hell's unwilling bride. Thus begins Persephone's struggle with loss and depression. As Jean Shinoda Bolen points out in her book *Goddesses in Everywoman*: "Symbolically, the underworld can represent deeper layers of the psyche, a place where memories and feelings have been 'buried' (the personal unconscious) and where images, patterns, instincts, and feelings that are archetypal and shared by humanity are found (the collective unconscious)." Persephone becomes extremely depressed, unable to eat or to see any end to her suffering.

For women, abduction takes many forms. But in all of them, something or someone with immeasurable value to us is lost; our health or our emotional or physical security is threatened; a friend betrays us; we have an abortion; lose a job; are divorced—these are just some of the circumstances that can cause an alteration in the way we experience reality. It can happen at any time in our lives. If you ever feel you don't know who you are; if you feel confused, without direction, lost, indecisive, trapped, alone, desolate, depressed, isolated, numb, disconnected, afraid, or hopeless—these feelings are common, and represent the dark, unenlightened side of yourself. In this stage of your journey, you can seem introverted, unable to be fully present. You may feel like a part of your self is somewhere else, and indeed it is. But, as Alice tells the Caterpillar, it is important to remember that this stage is only the beginning of a much larger journey:

> "BUT WHEN YOU HAVE TO TURN INTO A CHRYSALIS—
> YOU WILL SOME DAY, YOU KNOW—AND THEN AFTER
> THAT INTO A BUTTERFLY, I SHOULD THINK YOU'LL FEEL
> IT A LITTLE QUEER, WON'T YOU?"

When we are feeling bereft and depressed, we might blame outside circumstances for our suffering, just as Persephone blames Hades for her suffering. We see reality as unfair, cruel, and unjust; we can make no sense of the horrible things that are happening to us. We feel that nobody is there to respond to our cries for help, and that we are at the mercy of outside forces. We feel as Alice does—trapped.

So many young women today are "abducted" and "married to Hades" against their will. Countless women are the victims of rape and drug addiction, while some even attempt suicide. In fashion magazines, more and more women appear anorexic, lacking Aphrodite's beauty, joy, and radiance. They are under the delusion that they are "fashionably" thin, and thereby rationalize their refusal to eat.

But the myth of Persephone is really a myth of great hope. She comes out of the darkness into the light, and by so doing reminds us that the darkness isn't permanent. How does she do it? Endurance, acceptance, and surrender are her tools.

This return to joyfulness is the third stage of the journey. By partaking of the pomegranate seed, the fruit of knowledge, Persephone integrates the dark and the light parts of her life, which becomes her salvation. Persephone can never fully return to her innocence because she knows of the underworld, and she becomes responsible for what she knows. Unlike the other goddesses, Persephone mirrors our humanness through her transformational journey. The moment of Persephone's reconciliation with her mother is one of ecstasy, pure joy, and Demeter allows the earth to bloom again. Yet Persephone is forever changed because of her experience. The moment we emerge from the darkness of a long, painful struggle and reconnect with the light, experiencing the loving parts of ourself, is such an extraordinary triumph. It is then that we realize that our own resistance, our unwillingness to accept the way things happen, may have prolonged our suffering. The sooner we let go, the sooner liberation comes.

As we embrace, integrate, and accept our difficult experiences, we enter the fourth stage of our journey. Only then can we assist others toward enlightenment and offer them the gift of empathy. With them, we take command of our own strength and exercise our newfound wisdom. This is the stage when Persephone has grown up and assumes her full power, independent of her mother. She willingly agrees to return to Hades as his wife, completely embracing the dark side of herself, no longer afraid of her shadow. As Persephone grows into her role as queen of the underworld, she actually comes to love Hades. The story of Persephone shows us that nothing is ever really lost, and that we only learn this by experiencing it.

Hades comes to represent not just the underworld—something to be feared and avoided—he is also the god of wealth, and represents depth and the riches of understanding. These riches, residing deep within us, are not to be resisted, for they are the key to our metamorphosis. Because there is grace and wisdom in the surrender to transformation, we must come to embrace the experiences that abduct us from the cozy and predictable patterns of our lives and lead us to claim all the parts of our souls.

Free Your Unconscious Mind

✦ Write down your dreams on a regular basis and consider taking a dream interpretation course. Dreams can be a powerful means of accessing the unconscious, and once you unravel their mysteries they can enlighten you, guide you, and reveal answers to your most significant questions.

✦ Participate in a silent spiritual retreat. Listen to the voice that comes to you in the silence.

✦ Listen to music and allow it to touch your deepest feelings. You could start with Mozart's opera *The Magic Flute*, which tells the story of a mystical journey of transformation, or Vivaldi's *The Four Seasons*, which beautifully captures the journey from one season to the next.

✦ Practice expressing your innermost thoughts and feelings to a counselor or a friend whom you trust. Stream-of-consciousness writing is another way to allow your hidden feelings to be released.

Help Others Transform

✦ Spend quality time with your mother or a mother figure with whom you feel safe. The two of you might take a trip somewhere special, giving you both the opportunity to share your most intimate emotions.

◆ Volunteer at a hospice. Helping people with their transition from this world to the next might assist you in overcoming your own fears—of living *and* of dying.

◆ Become a "big sister" to someone younger than you.

CULTIVATE THE ART OF ACCEPTANCE

◆ Listen carefully to what others have to say. A receptive attitude to others can help you develop receptivity toward your own psyche.

◆ Kindness toward yourself can also help you through a difficult phase. Remember—your value is independent of your feelings.

A Literary Reflection

Persephone

WHEN THEY CALLED ME TO COME DOWN AND RIDE THE RED PALANQUIN, I WAS SITTING AT A SMALL DRESSING TABLE BY AN OPEN WINDOW. I BEGAN TO CRY AND THOUGHT BITTERLY ABOUT MY PARENTS' PROMISE. I WONDERED WHY MY DESTINY HAD BEEN DECIDED, WHY I SHOULD HAVE AN UNHAPPY LIFE SO SOMEONE ELSE COULD HAVE A HAPPY ONE. FROM MY SEAT BY THE WINDOW I COULD SEE THE FEN RIVER WITH ITS MUDDY BROWN WATERS. I THOUGHT ABOUT THROWING MY BODY INTO THIS RIVER THAT HAD DESTROYED MY FAMILY'S HAPPINESS. A PERSON HAS VERY STRANGE THOUGHTS WHEN IT SEEMS THAT LIFE IS ABOUT TO END.

IT STARTED TO RAIN AGAIN, JUST A LIGHT RAIN. THE PEOPLE FROM DOWNSTAIRS CALLED UP TO ME ONCE AGAIN TO HURRY. AND MY THOUGHTS BECAME MORE URGENT, MORE STRANGE.

I ASKED MYSELF, WHAT IS TRUE ABOUT A PERSON? WOULD I CHANGE IN THE SAME WAY THE RIVER CHANGES COLOR BUT STILL BE THE SAME PERSON? AND THEN I SAW THE CURTAINS BLOWING WILDLY, AND OUTSIDE RAIN WAS FALLING HARDER, CAUSING EVERYONE TO SCURRY AND SHOUT. I SMILED. AND THEN I REALIZED IT WAS THE FIRST TIME I COULD SEE THE POWER OF THE WIND. I COULDN'T SEE THE WIND ITSELF, BUT I COULD SEE IT CARRIED THE WATER THAT FILLED THE RIVERS AND SHAPED THE COUNTRYSIDE. IT CAUSED MEN TO YELP AND DANCE.

I WIPED MY EYES AND LOOKED IN THE MIRROR. I

WAS SURPRISED AT WHAT I SAW. I HAD ON A BEAUTI-
FUL RED DRESS, BUT WHAT I SAW WAS EVEN MORE
VALUABLE. I WAS STRONG. I WAS PURE. I HAD GENUINE
THOUGHTS INSIDE THAT NO ONE COULD SEE, THAT NO
ONE COULD EVER TAKE AWAY FROM ME. I WAS LIKE THE
WIND.

I THREW MY HEAD BACK AND SMILED PROUDLY TO
MYSELF. AND THEN I DRAPED THE LARGE EMBROI-
DERED RED SCARF OVER MY FACE AND COVERED THESE
THOUGHTS UP. BUT UNDERNEATH THE SCARF I STILL
KNEW WHO I WAS. I MADE A PROMISE TO MYSELF: I
WOULD ALWAYS REMEMBER MY PARENTS' WISHES, BUT
I WOULD NEVER FORGET MYSELF . . .

SOMEONE TOOK MY HANDS AND GUIDED ME DOWN
A PATH. I WAS LIKE A BLIND PERSON WALKING TO MY
FATE. BUT I WAS NO LONGER SCARED. I COULD SEE
WHAT WAS INSIDE ME.

—Lindo Jong, a bride in an arranged marriage, in
Amy Tan's *The Joy Luck Club*

CREDITS

WORKS OF ART

13, 16–17 Sandro Botticelli, *The Birth of Venus*, 1482
Uffizi Gallery, Florence, Italy
Photograph © Scala/Art Resource, NY

24–25 Titian, *Venus of Urbino*, 1538
Uffizi Gallery, Florence, Italy
Photograph © Scala/Art Resource, NY

33 Sir Edward Burne-Jones, *The Mirror of Venus*, 1898
Gulbenkian Museum, Lisbon, Portugal
Photograph © Scala/Art Resource, NY

35, 39 School of Fontainebleau, *Diana as Huntress*,
ca. 1550, Louvre, Paris, France
Photograph © Scala/Art Resource, NY

46 *Diana*, fresco from a villa in Stabia, ca. 50 B.C.
National Museum of Archaeology, Naples, Italy
Photograph © Scala/Art Resource, NY

51 *Athena Promachos* (Roman copy after Greek original of
the 5th century B.C.), from the Villa dei Papiri or
Villa dei Pisoni, Herculaneum, 1st century B.C.,
National Museum of Archaeology, Naples, Italy
Photograph © Nimatallah/Art Resource, NY

64–65 Jacopo Tintoretto, *Athena and Arachne*, 1579
Contini-Bonacossi Collection, Florence, Italy
Photograph © Scala/Art Resource, NY

69, 72–73 Jan the Elder Brueghel, *Ceres and
the Four Elements*, 1604
Kunsthistorisches Museum, Vienna, Austria
Photograph © Erich Lessing/Art Resource, NY

86, back cover Raphael, fresco depicting Venus with
Ceres and Juno, 1517, from a spandrel of the
Psyche Loggia Palazzo della Farnesina, Rome, Italy
Photograph © Scala/Art Resource, NY

89, 100–101 Andrea Appiani, *The Toilette of Juno*,
ca. late 17th century
Pinacoteca Civica, Brescia, Italy
Photograph © Scala/Art Resource, NY

105 Peter Paul Rubens, *Henri IV Receiving the Portrait of
Maria de' Medici*, (Maria de' Medici cycle), ca. 1620
Louvre, Paris, France
Photograph © Giraudon/Art Resource, NY

109, 118 *Cup of Oltos*, depicting the reunion of
the Gods (Zeus served by Ganymede, Hestia,
and Aphrodite), ca. 500 B.C.
Archaeological Museum, Tarquinia, Italy
Photograph © Nimatallah/Art Resource, NY

111 Francesco Albani, *Fire*, from a series depicting the
Four Elements, 17th century
Galleria Sabauda, Turin, Italy
Photograph © Alinari/Art Resource, NY

123, 126–27 Sandro Botticelli, *Primavera*, 1477–78
Uffizi Gallery, Florence, Italy
Photograph © Scala/Art Resource, NY

133 Dante Gabriel Rossetti, *Proserpine*, 1874
Tate Gallery, London, England
Photograph © Tate Gallery/Art Resource, NY

Back cover flap: photograph by Vangelis Kyris

NUMBERS PRECEDING ENTRIES REFER TO PAGE NUMBERS.

5   Emily Dickinson, "We never know how high we are." Reprinted by permission of the Harvard College Library, from *The Poems of Emily Dickinson*, Thomas H. Johnson, ed. (Cambridge, Mass.: Belknap Press of Harvard University Press, 1983), in *Return of the Goddess: An Engagement Calendar for 1997*, Burleigh Mutén, ed. (New York: Stewart, Tabori & Chang, 1997).

10   Joseph Campbell, *The Power of Myth* (New York: Bantam Doubleday Dell Publishing Group, 1988), pp. 5, 39.

12   George Bernard Shaw, *The Apple Cart: A Political Extravaganza* (New York: Penguin Books, 1983), pp. 89–90. Courtesy of The Society of Authors, on behalf of the Bernard Shaw Estate.

14   Second Homeric Hymn to Aphrodite, trans. by Jules Cashford. *Harvest: Journal for Jungian Studies*, vol. 33, (1987–88), pp. 204–7. Quoted in Anne Baring and Jules Cashford, *The Myth of the Goddess: Evolution of an Image* (New York: Penguin Books, 1991), p. 351.

22   Emily Dickinson, "Valentine Week." Reprinted by permission of the Harvard College Library, from *The Poems of Emily Dickinson*, Thomas H. Johnson, ed. (Cambridge, Mass.: Belknap Press of Harvard University Press, 1983), p. 3.

23   D. H. Lawrence, *Lady Chatterley's Lover* (New York: Grove Press, Inc., 1928), pp. 183–84.

26   Mirabai, untitled poem, in *Women in Praise of the Sacred: Forty-Three Centuries of Spiritual Poetry by Women*, Jane Hirshfield, ed. (New York: HarperCollins Publishers, 1995), p. 138.

26–27   Lucille Clifton, "homage to my hips." Copyright © 1980 by Lucille Clifton. Now appears in *Good Woman*, (Boa Editions, Ltd.). Reprinted by permission of Curtis Brown, Ltd.

28   Jeannine Dominy, screenplay entitled "The Honest Courtesan," released as the film *Dangerous Beauty*, 1998.

34   George Bernard Shaw, *The Apple Cart: A Political Extravaganza* (New York: Penguin Books, 1983), pp. 89–91. Courtesy of The Society of Authors, on behalf of the Bernard Shaw Estate.

36   Aeschylus, *Agamemnon*, in *The Oresteian Trilogy*, trans. by Philip Vellacott (Harmondsworth, England: Penguin Books, 1959), p. 133. Quoted in Anne Baring and Jules Cashford, *The Myth of the Goddess: Evolution of an Image* (New York: Penguin Books, 1991), p. 321.

37   Homer, *Odyssey*, trans. by E. V. Rieu (Harmondsworth, England: Penguin Books, 1946), pp. 6, 102–8. Quoted in Anne Baring and Jules Cashford, *The Myth of the Goddess: Evolution of an Image* (New York: Penguin Books, 1991), p. 322.

37–38   Robert Graves, *The Greek Myths*, vol. I (London: Penguin Books, 1960), p. 22.

44   George Bernard Shaw, *Misalliance: A Debate in One Sitting* (New York: Samuel French, Inc., 1914), p. 215. Copyright © 1957, The Public Trustee as executor of the estate of George Bernard Shaw. Courtesy of The Society of Authors, on behalf of the Bernard Shaw Estate.

45   Amelia Earhart, "Courage," in Doris L. Rich, *Amelia Earhart: A Biography* (Washington: Smithsonian Institution Press, 1989), pp. 48–49.

47   Eleanor Roosevelt, quoted in Deborah G. Felder, *The One Hundred Most Influential Women of All Time: A Ranking Past and Present* (New York: Carol Publishing Group, 1996), p. 3.

50   George Bernard Shaw, *Misalliance: A Debate in One Sitting* (New York: Samuel French, Inc., 1914), pp. 215–16. Copyright © 1957, The Public Trustee as executor of the estate of George Bernard Shaw. Courtesy of The Society of Authors, on behalf of the Bernard Shaw Estate.

52–53 Homeric Hymn to Artemis, trans. by Jules Cashford. *Harvest: Journal for Jungian Studies*, vol. 33, (1987–88), pp. 204–7. Quoted in Anne Baring and Jules Cashford, *The Myth of the Goddess: Evolution of an Image* (New York: Penguin Books, 1991), p. 321.

54 Homer, *Odyssey*, trans. by Moses Hadas. Quoted in W. F. Otto, *The Homeric Gods: The Spiritual Significance of Greek Religion* (London: Thames and Hudson, 1954), p. 46.

58 Aeschylus, *The Eumenides*, trans. by Robert Sagles. Quoted in Arianna Huffington and Roloff Beny, *The Gods of Greece* (New York: Harry N. Abrams, Inc., Publishers, 1983), p. 141.

59 Henrik Ibsen, *A Doll's House*, adapted by Frank McGuinness (New York: Dramatists Play Service, Inc., 1998), p. 64.

61 Nina Berberova, interview with Kennedy Fraser, in *Ornament and Silence: Essays on Women's Lives* (New York: Alfred A. Knopf, Inc.,1997), pp. 24–25.

62 Florence Nightingale, *Cassandra*. Quoted in *A Woman Speaks: Women Famous, Infamous, and Unknown*, compiled by Lydia Cosentino (Rancho Mirage, Calif.: Dramaline Publications, 1995), p. 118.

62–63 George Bernard Shaw, *Saint Joan* (New York: W. W. Norton & Company, 1914), p. 215. Copyright © 1957, The Public Trustee as executor of the estate of George Bernard Shaw. Courtesy of The Society of Authors, on behalf of the Bernard Shaw Estate.

63 Susan B. Anthony, 1872 speech. Quoted in *A Woman Speaks: Women Famous, Infamous, and Unknown*, compiled by Lydia Cosentino (Rancho Mirage, Calif.: Dramaline Publications, 1995), p. 20.

68 William Shakespeare, *The Merchant of Venice*, in *The Complete Works of William Shakespeare: Comprising His Plays and Poems* (London: The Hamlyn Publishing Group, Ltd., 1958), p. 203.

70–71 Hesiod, *Theogony and Works and Days*, trans. by Dorothea Wender (Harmondsworth, England: Penguin Books, 1973), pp. 969–71. Quoted in Anne Baring and Jules Cashford, *The Myth of the Goddess: Evolution of an Image* (New York: Penguin Books, 1991), p. 366.

71 Homeric Hymn to Demeter, trans. by Jules Cashford. Quoted in Anne Baring and Jules Cashford, *The Myth of the Goddess: Evolution of an Image* (New York: Penguin Books, 1991), p. 371.

79 C. G. Jung, "The Psychological Aspects of the Kore," in *Essays on a Science of Mythology* (Princeton: Princeton University Press, 1969). Quoted in Arianna Huffington and Roloff Beny, *The Gods of Greece* (New York: Harry N. Abrams, Inc., Publishers, 1983), p. 178.

80–81 Kahlil Gibran, *Jesus, the Son of Man: His Words and His Deeds as Told and Recorded by Those Who Knew Him*. Copyright © 1928 by Kahlil Gibran and renewed 1956 by Administrators C.T.A. of Kahlil Gibran Estate and Mary G. Gibran. (New York: Alfred A. Knopf, Inc., 1956), p. 94. Reprinted by permission of Alfred A. Knopf, Inc. and Gibran National Committee.

82 Isabel Allende, *Paula* (New York: HarperCollins Publishers, 1996), p. 330.

87–88 Colette, *Break of Day*, trans. by Enid McLeod. (London: Martin Secker and Warburg Ltd, 1961), pp. 5–6. Reprinted by permission of Farrar, Straus and Giroux, LLC.

92 Robert Graves, *The Greek Myths*, vol. 2 (London: Penguin Books, 1960), p. 11.

93 Homer, *The Orphic Hymns*, trans. by Apostolos N. Athanassakis (Missoula, Montana: Scholars Press, 1977), p. 27.

97–98 Judy Chicago, *The Dinner Party* (New York: Anchor Press, 1979), p. 167. Quoted in Jennifer Barker Woolger and Roger J. Woolger, *The Goddess Within: A Guide to the Eternal Myths that Shape Women's Lives* (New York: Ballantine Books, 1989), p. 193.

98 Joseph Campbell, *The Power of Myth* (New York: Bantam Doubleday Dell Publishing Group, 1988), pp. 6–7.

99 Sally Kempton, "Cutting Loose" (*Esquire* magazine, July 1970, © Hearst Communications, Inc.). Quoted in Viveca Lindfors and Paul Austin, *I Am a Woman: The Journey of One Woman and Many Women* (New York: Applause Theater Book Publishers, 1990), pp. 20–21.

103 Joseph Campbell, *The Power of Myth* (New York: Bantam Doubleday Dell Publishing Group, 1988), p. 6.

103 Federico Fellini, *Fellini on Fellini* (New York: New Directions, 1976), p. 83. Quoted in Jennifer Barker Woolger and Roger J. Woolger, *The Goddess Within: A Guide to the Eternal Myths that Shape Women's Lives* (New York: Ballantine Books, 1989), p. 220.

104 Kahlil Gibran, *The Prophet.* © 1923 by Kahlil Gibran and renewed 1951 by Administrators C.T.A. of Kahlil Gibran Estate and Mary G. Gibran. (New York: Alfred A. Knopf, Inc., 1998), pp. 15–16. Reprinted by permission of Alfred A. Knopf, Inc. and Gibran National Committee.

108 William Shakespeare, *Julius Caesar*, in *The Complete Works of William Shakespeare: Comprising His Plays and Poems* (London: The Hamlyn Publishing Group, Ltd., 1958), p. 727.

110 Robert Graves, *The Greek Myths*, vol. 1 (London: Penguin Books, 1960), p. 75.

116 Joseph Campbell, *The Power of Myth* (New York: Bantam Doubleday Dell Publishing Group, 1988), p. 92.

117 Elsa Gidlow, "Chains of Fire." Quoted in *Return of the Goddess: An Engagement Calendar for 1997*, Burleigh Mutén, ed. (New York: Stewart, Tabori & Chang, 1997).

117–19 Mother Teresa, *In the Heart of the World: Thoughts, Stories, and Prayers* (Novato, Calif.: New World Library, 1997), pp. 20–21.

119 Rainer Maria Rilke, *Selected Poems of Rainer Maria Rilke*, trans. by Robert Bly (New York: HarperCollins Publishers, 1981), p. 70. Quoted in *In Praise of Women*, Jonathan Meader, ed. (Berkeley, Calif.: Celestial Arts, 1997), p. 70.

122 Fyodor Dostoyevsky, untitled poem, in Elizabeth Roberts and Elias Amidon, eds., *Life Prayers from Around the World* (New York: HarperCollins Publishers, 1996), p. 26.

124–25 Homeric Hymn to Demeter, trans. by Jules Cashford. Quoted in Anne Baring and Jules Cashford, *The Myth of the Goddess: Evolution of an Image* (New York: Penguin Books, 1991), p. 370.

132 Lewis Carroll, *Alice's Adventures in Wonderland and Through the Looking-Glass and What Alice Found There* (Rutland, Vermont: Charles E. Tuttle Company, Inc., 1998), p. 39.

134 Jean Giraudoux, *The Enchanted*, in *Jean Giraudoux: Four Plays*, adapted and with an introduction by Maurice Valency (New York: Hill and Wang, 1986), p. 166.

134 Jean Shinoda Bolen, *Goddesses in Everywoman: A New Psychology of Women* (New York: HarperCollins Publishers, 1985), p. 202.

135 Lewis Carroll, *Alice's Adventures in Wonderland and Through the Looking-Glass and What Alice Found There* (Rutland, Vermont: Charles E. Tuttle Company, Inc., 1998), p. 41.

139–40 Amy Tan, *The Joy Luck Club* (New York: G.P. Putnam's Sons, 1989), pp. 52–54.